MAKE SUPER PROFITS IN ANY ECONOMY

Master the Seven Secrets of the Super Brands

WILLIS AMACH

HEZMA VENTURES

Unless indicated otherwise, all quotes used in this book have been taken from the Brainy Quotes website https://www.brainyquote.com

ISBN-13: 978-9966-8275-3-1

Cover design by: Hezma Ventures

Printed in Kenya

CONTENTS

INTRODUCTION

In every industry there are a few insanely successful enterprises that consistently dominate the market, make super sales turnovers and record profitability that defy the prevailing economic conditions. These brands have achieved market distinctions by being truly differentiated from the competition; they have become well known for consistently offering high quality products and superior services; they can be relied upon to deliver on their promises.

This group of enterprises is composed of the industry super achievers that have successfully weathered the storms of the business world and emerged as the industry titans and dominant pacesetters to boot. They have effectively crowded out the competition and remained to play in their own leagues.

Interestingly, this elite league of the super achievers is not limited either by industry or geography; on the contrary such brands can and do blossom in almost every geographical location and industry imaginable.

The customers of these super brands have effectively become their loyal brand ambassadors freely advertising their superb experiences in their circles of influence and thus effectively creating new customers.

Additionally, these elite businesses easily attract investors who are eager to buy a stake in them. They also get more opportunities for investments and partnerships and thereby easily expanding their outreach and presence into new territories.

As these titans seem to have it all easy, *"taking all the customers"* and making all the money, the rest of the businesses are apparently caught up in epic and draining struggles just to get by with very little or nothing to show for their efforts.

What are these super brands doing so differently that gives them the excellent results that seems so elusive to the remaining market players? What is so *magical* about these super achievers that give them such market dominance?

We submit to you respectfully ladies and gentlemen that after doing extensive studies on these super achievers, we have established that these industry titans have certain *secrets* or *pillars* in common that ensure their success no matter the prevailing economic circumstances.

Moreover, we have also noted that the collective and faithful application of these secrets enable these businesses to build and sustain well-oiled product and service delivery machineries to a growing pool of their satisfied and evangelical customers, with an exactness that can be replicated.

After taking a deep dive into the world of the super achieving brands and going behind the scenes to unmask their hitherto hidden business ingredients, we now reveal these secrets of the movers and shakers of the various industries to all the budding entrepreneurs and business leaders alike in one book.

We bring to the fore in one collection what has being confidential information of the super achievers; we unveil the secrets that the industry titans employ so effectively to dominate the markets and stay ahead of the pack while they leave the vast majority of businesses to scramble for a space in whatever '*little*' they have left.

You will be delighted to learn that these leading brands are not leading by chance; on the contrary they have mastered and perfected the art and science of doing business in a manner that is guaranteed to produce immense returns in a sustainable way.

These business *secrets* deployed by the super brands have both been tested and proven time and again to strike a positive code with the target customers and effectively win their hearts and minds and hence their continued patronage, thus propelling the respective brands to positions of market dominance.

Now you too can purpose to join this elite league of the super achievers by utilizing these *secrets* or *pillars* in your business or organization, and stand to enjoy the immense rewards that come with it.

The good news is that you do not have to re-invent the wheel; you can simply take cues from the best practices that the super brands have adopted that make them to thrive regardless of the state of the economy and in the face of cut-throat competition.

The second good news is that these super brands do not employ any magical or mysterious means to *hold their markets hostage*; on the contrary they simply approach and carry out their business operations differently using these time-tested secrets with utmost fidelity and consummate devotion.

•••

In this book, we lay bare these ingredients that we have carefully studied and hereby presents to you as **The Seven Secrets** or **The Seven Pillars of the super brands**.

The seven pillars cover the whole spectrum of best practices, underlying principles and wholesome policies that leading brands religiously employ in their day-to-day operations and long term strategies to stay ahead of the pack.

Join us as we take this exhilarating journey of discoveries that will shake off some of your long held limiting beliefs and excitedly usher you into the world and mindset of the super achievers.

We shall share some very unsettling truths, unravel some paradoxes and challenge you to embrace some time-tested empowering ideologies in your businesses going forward.

The hidden theme

To help you get the most value out of this book as we explore each of the seven pillars, we shall keep referring to an underlying theme that all these pillars or ingredients feed and work together to achieve. We will not mention the theme directly but shall give you valuable clues on every chapter to enable you to discover it on your own.

You might discover the hidden theme on your first reading or even on your third reading of this book. Once you get and embrace it, you will be on your way to transforming your business and setting it on the path of joining the league of the super brands.

We have included some reflection questions at the end of each chapter to provoke your thoughts and get you into the action mode. You can discuss these questions with your teams or meditate through them individually to honestly gauge your current business circumstances with a view to taking appropriate steps to address any apparent gaps therein.

Seize the moment, transform the DNA of your business and reap big financial returns in a sustainable way. Let the journey begin.

CHAPTER ONE: PURPOSE

Fidelity to a worthy purpose

"There is one quality which one must possess to win, and that is definiteness of purpose, the knowledge of what one wants, and a burning desire to possess it."

~NAPOLEON HILL

A great journey starts with an exciting destination in mind. Even if it is the first trip ever to the particular destination, the travellers will at least have an inkling of the place even if only by name and the direction thereof; moreover the travellers usually form some mental pictures of the destination and what it portends for their lives.

In the context of a business entity, the journey with an exciting destination in mind is the core purpose of the business. This is the first thing that leading brands get clear on as they start off.

The only difference however is that in business this exciting destination is almost always a place where the travelers have only gone to mentally but which nonetheless is not only enticing but also promises better prospects than their current circumstances.

In pursuit of a noble purpose

The adventures of the great souls behind every super brand is fuelled by a burning desire to bring workable solutions to real problems affecting the society; they always seek to either find better ways of addressing the pain points of certain constituencies within the society or to offer cheaper alternatives to resolving lingering societal issues.

These journeys seldom have anything to do with the personal financial gains of the specific individuals concerned. To illustrate this point, we will look at three examples in living memory:

1) *Two young men aged 19 and 21 years respectively met in college in 2003 and soon realized that they had similar aspirations to create a centralized website that could enable university students to connect and share ideas. They observed that the university neither had such a website nor the plans to put one in place any sooner.*

   They then worked together to resolve the issue at hand and Facebook was born one year later.

   This is the story of Mark Elliot Zuckerberg and his co-founder Eduardo Saverin who were both students at Harvard University at the time.

2) *Two students from totally different backgrounds met at Stanford University's PhD program in 1995 and as fate would have it, they found themselves working together on a research project entitled "The Anatomy of a Large-Scale Hypertextual Web Search Engine."*

This joint research paper became the basis for Google Inc. which was later founded by the duo three years later. This is the story of Larry Page and Sergey Brin.

3) *In 1994, a 30 year old executive in a Wall Street investment company, D.E Shaw & Co. left his lucrative job and six-figure salary to embark on a journey that would see him build the largest online retail company in the world.*

Fueled with a burning passion to build an e-commerce platform that could enable people everywhere on the globe to buy and sell items online, he ventured into the unchartered waters of the World Wide Web to try his hands on the infant business of online retailing.

And the move paid off.

This is the story of Jeff Bezos the founder of Amazon Inc. and as they say, the rest is history.

We could give other examples of such great journeys that have disrupted the markets and re-shaped the world.

They are journeys in pursuit of noble purposes, to solve real problems in the society and make the world a better place.

This brings us to the first secret of the super brands:

the pursuit of a worthy purpose.

Simply put, the first pillar that separates every super brand from the vast average majority companies is their *singular fidelity to a clear, compelling and a worthy purpose.*

At the core of every great brand is a higher order reason that defines the brand's existence.

Purpose is the WHY of a business existence; the main reason why the brand was founded in the first place, why it continues to operate and what significance or value it adds to its customers.

In this book, we define purpose of a business as:

> *The essence or the core reason for a brand's existence that adds value to the society and goes beyond the need to make money for the shareholders*

Leading brands uphold fidelity to their purposes and use their purpose statements to drive their mission and achieve their broad objectives.

A great business purpose is one that supersedes the need to make money. As Silicon Valley venture capitalist and author Guy Takeo Kawasaki aptly remarked:

> *"Great companies start because the founders want to change the world, not make a fast buck"*

Every great organization is essentially built on a solid foundation of a worthy purpose, whose primary aim is to solve a real problem in the society, or to address particular pain points of the target customers. *It is never about making more money or becoming rich.*

The founders of these organizations are driven by a noble desire to bring a valuable solution to a definite problem in the society and to make a difference in the world. The primary focus of this category of business founders is the welfare of their target customers as opposed to lining their own pockets.

They therefore craft a purpose statement that serves as the company's *True North* on the business magnetic compass to guide the actions of every member of the company from the chief executive officer down to the cleaner.

The purpose statement does not only guide the company members in the filtering of their daily decisions but also in providing a collective understanding of what they are supposed to accomplish.

In addition to bringing workable solutions to the target customers' pain points, worthy purpose also entail bringing more conveniences to the target consumers by providing superior but cheaper alternatives to their current ways of operations.

◆ ◆ ◆

Why Your Business Needs A Clear And Compelling Purpose

In order to successfully weather the storms of the business environment, a business needs to have a compelling and clear purpose.

Definiteness of purpose has been recognized by world leaders as a key ingredient for success in any endeavor in life. This truth becomes only more pronounced in the world of business.

Every great brand upholds fidelity to a clear and a compelling purpose that serves as the lenses through which the company members see and interact with the world.

American motivational speaker and best-selling author of the audio series *The Psychology of Winning,* Denis Waitley said that:

> *"Winners are people with definite purpose in life"*

Moreover, it has been noted by thought leaders and pioneer business moguls that if you stay in your course long enough in the pursuit of a noble purpose you begin to attract 'luck' in your life; you begin to encounter more lucky opportunities; you begin to attract the right people and resources that are necessary to achieve your goals. That's why Ralph Waldo Emerson noted that:

"Good luck is another name for tenacity of purpose"

A powerful and worthy purpose is a force that is unbeatable by anything else in the world. It not only attracts and retains top talent in the market, but it also serves as a magnet for strategic investors who willingly partners with the particular brand as it pursues its growth objectives.

In addition, a strong purpose unites the members of an establishment and compels them to create, explore and discover new ways of providing the desired outcomes to their customers.

In this sense, purpose serves as the pivotal point of aspiration that generates enthusiasm and creativity among the members of the organization, as they are persuaded that their work is not only meaningful but also makes a real difference in the world.

Even more importantly, a worthy purpose is attractive to customers who feel morally obliged to support such brands by offering their continued patronage. The customers become evangelical and fiercely loyal to these brands to the exclusion of any other.

Nothing is as powerful and richly rewarding as having an army of loyal customers turned fans freely advocating your brand within their circles of influence.

Some super brands such as the Coca-Cola Company and Equity Group Holdings have specifically spelt out their powerful purpose statements and put the same in the public domain, while others such as Amazon Inc. and Google Inc. have their purpose captured within their broader mission statements.

Examples of all-time best purpose statements

Let's take a look at three examples of the all-time best purpose statements that revolutionized the world and made the companies super brands, effectively disrupting their industries and re-defining customers' experiences:

1. "To bring inspiration and innovation to every athlete in the world"[1]

This was the original purpose statement of Nike Inc. a super brand company that specializes in the manufacture of sports gear.

That statement is loaded with very powerful objectives and insanely audacious ambition; the purpose statement gave the company the impetus to do everything and anything possible to expand human potential in all matters concerning sports.

In a nutshell, the above purpose statement clarified that Nike Inc. targets *every* athlete in the world as a potential customer; this implied that the company did not envision any geographical barriers in its market outreach. This purpose statement effectively gave Nike Inc. the leeway to either create new markets or to deeply penetrate existing ones.

For the avoidance of doubt, Nike's purpose as captured in the statement was not limited to making sports shoes but any sports gear that would inspire and bring out the best in every athlete.

By the way, according to Nike Inc. every single person in the world is a potential athlete. Nike avers that *"if you have a body, you are an athlete."*[2]

This purpose statement has since been revised to incorporate the envisaged impact of Nike Inc. in the world through sports. The expanded statement is equally audacious and truly glamorous. Here is the new Nike Inc. purpose statement:

Our purpose is to unite the world through sport to create a healthy planet, active communities and an equal playing field for all.[3]

2. "To help people save money so they can live better"[4]

This is the purpose statement of Walmart, the US giant retailer. The statement is so simple and yet so powerful.

Walmart's focus is to help the masses to save money as they make their purchases and as a result thereof they can live better lives.

A noble and social aspiration is captured in that simple statement. It is evident that it has worked wonders judging by the millions of masses that troop into Walmart stores on a weekly basis to *'save money'* and *'live better'* that has effectively propelled the brand to global dominance in the retail industry.

3. "To make a contribution to the world by making tools for the mind that advance humankind"[5]

This was the purpose statement of Apple Inc. under the leadership of the late Steve Jobs. The statement is packed with so much ambition, so much determination on such a grand scale.

Jobs considered Apple's products as tools for improving the quality of life for mankind, and designed them as such.

That original purpose statement was instrumental in attracting top talent and inspiring great creativity and innovation at Apple Inc. that effectively propelled the company to global dominance in the computing technology industry under the leadership of the late Steve Jobs.

The statement has since been revised to *"to empower creative exploration and self-expression"[6]* to reflect the changing business trends under Apple's new leadership.

We hope you get the gist of it.

In a nutshell, in order to become great, a business brand needs a strong purpose capable of uniting its members in productive creativity and quality innovations that resonates well with the market.

Furthermore, the business purpose should be fiercely customer-centric and empowering in its execution if it is to enable a brand to break through to the elite league of the super achievers and cause formidable ripples in the market.

◆ ◆ ◆

What Is Your Business Purpose?

Maybe you need to ask yourself whether your business has a known purpose that it serves in the market in the first place, and whether that purpose is strong enough to attract the vital support from potential partners and secure the patronage of the targeted customers.

In case your answers to the above reflective questions are negative, worry no more. The information contained in this book will help you to get your business purpose right.

To start with, you will need to peel back the many layers of your daily engagements and get to the core of why you are in business in the first place.

In the midst of the many transactions and deals your business is currently engaged in or aspires to engage in, you need to ask yourself whether they are all designed to achieve a given known purpose beyond just closing sales and bringing in more revenue for your company.

You need to ascertain and be clear on the specific benefits your customers get as a result of consuming your products and services. You need to be clear on the specific desired outcome your customers receive on consuming your products and services. Lastly you need to do introspection and confirm that your products and services as currently designed are delivering that desired outcome to your customers.

Every transaction or business a company is engaged in serves to either further its cause or actively veto the same, there is no neutrality in matters business and purpose.

When the core reason or essence of the business is not properly defined as is the case with many businesses, it is easier to get sidetracked or swayed by the many competing interests as the business essentially lacks an anchor to keep it firmly grounded or on track.

When purpose of an object or something is not clarified or is unknown, abuse becomes inevitable. For a business that is unclear on its brand's purpose, misuse or misallocation of resources inadvertently takes center stage; confusion, wastage and pilferage of company resources easily becomes the norm rather than the exception in such a setting that is devoid of corporate focus.

It therefore behooves the leadership of every business to both identify and clearly define the corporate purpose that their business is serving in the marketplace. This is the first laudable step on the journey to achieving brand greatness.

Once you get clear on your business purpose, it is time to put it down in a relatable but powerful and inspiring statement. Such a statement shall serve to clarify your company purpose to both the company members and the external constituencies.

With relevant examples hereunder, we will show you how you too can craft a powerful purpose statement to start off your company on the journey to achieving greatness.

Rules For Crafting Powerful Purpose Statements

Below are some rules for crafting powerful purpose statements:

- *Clearly communicate your WHY*

- *It must be customer-centric*

- *Make it inspiring*

- *Make it specific and differentiated*

- *It must have creative tension*

- *Make it both brief and memorable*

Let us explore the above points:

a) Clearly communicate your WHY

Every great undertaking starts with a definite and clearly defined WHY. This gives the people charged with the execution of the same both the impetus and the staying power to follow through with their assignment in spite of the changing circumstances and/or any other contingencies.

More than anything else, a purpose statement is all about the overarching reason why a brand exists. This core reason should therefore be clearly described in the purpose statement, anything short of this means that the statement has missed its *'purpose'*.

This is more so since the brand's purpose is more outward looking than inward looking. In other words, it seeks to communicate to the target customers and every other external constituency the reason for the brand's existence and the envisaged impact the business seeks to have on the customers.

It should be noted that the emphasis of a corporate purpose statement is not primarily on the products and services the company sells to the customers, on the contrary the focus is on the reason why the company is offering those products and services in the first place; in other words, it is about the expected outcome or benefits received from the consumption of the company products and services.

Take for example the purpose statement of Nike Inc. above:

> *"Our purpose is to unite the world through sport to create a healthy planet, active communities and an equal playing field for all"*

Nike Inc. manufactures sports gear for athletes but the same is not mentioned at all in the purpose statement; instead Nike talks about why they are in the business of making the sports gear—*to **unite** the world, create a **healthy planet** and **active** communities, to create an equal playing field (emphasis added in bold).* The making of cutting-edge sports gear is the means of serving that purpose.

b) It must be customer-centric

Every thriving business primarily operates for the benefit of the customers. In such firms the shareholders' interests are subordinate to the core mission designed to give the customers' superior experience with the brand.

The purpose statement should be crafted to strategically communicate the desired outcome for the target customers. This is because a brand's purpose statement not only communicates to the employees of the organization but even more importantly it communicates to the customers—both current and potential.

The message should therefore be intentionally crafted with the relevant target audience in mind. More specifically it must convey the benefits the target customers are to reap from the consumption of the brand's products and services.

It should be clear to the customers that the company exists to serve them and for their benefits primarily.

Let's look at these two examples.

Example One:

> *"Transforming lives, giving dignity and expanding opportunities for wealth creation"*[7]

The above is the purpose statement for Equity Group Holdings. Though a bit long but it communicates that all the work the banking conglomerate and all its subsidiaries is engaged in is intended to transform the lives of their customers, to give them dignity and opportunities to create wealth.

In a nutshell, all Equity Group Holdings' products are designed and developed exclusively to give their customers the above stated benefits.

The second example is here:

> *"To organize the world's information and make it universally accessible and useful"*

Can you guess which brand this is?

It is Google Inc. The giant technology company's core purpose is to organize the world's information and make it both **useful** and **accessible** from anywhere in the world for the benefit of its customers.

In pursuit of this noble purpose, Google Inc. has developed proprietary algorithms to maximize its effectiveness in organizing online information. Today if you want information on virtually anything, you just *google it* on the internet and you are sorted.

c) Make it inspiring

A great purpose statement serves as the spark that ignites productivity in the company and keeps the engine running.

The purpose statement of all leading brands serves as the pivotal point for the rallying call to all their team members to make their valuable contributions towards a common worthy cause.

All staff members should feel a sense of aliveness within their beings as they make their contributions towards the attainment of the brand's purpose.

Consider Apple Inc. purpose statement under Steve Jobs leadership as an example:

> *"To make a contribution to the world by making tools for the mind that advance humankind"*[5]

The above purpose statement spells such audacious and inspiring ambition, so much determination on such a grand scale. Apple Inc. aspired to see the **advancement** of humankind through the production of state-of-the-art technology devices.

Being a part of Apple team under Steve Jobs in whatever capacity as the company pursued its noble purpose brought inspiration and motivation to the staff, confident in the knowledge that their work played a significant role albeit in a small way, in delivering the state-of-the-art tech devices that transformed the world.

Let us look at a second example. The purpose statement of the giant soft-drink manufacturer, The Coca-Cola Company:

> *"Refresh the World. Make a difference"*[8]

So brief yet so loaded with meaning and inspiringly ambitious.

Coca-Cola exists to *refresh the world* and make a difference —no geographical, economic or ethnic boundaries are envisaged in the pursuit of this purpose.

This bold purpose has taken Coca-Cola products to every part of the world and made Coca-Cola part and parcel of every large celebration anywhere in the world today.

d) Make it specific and differentiated

Every super brand crafts a unique and differentiated purpose statement in response to the specific pain points or societal challenges they seek to resolve.

The world is unfortunately full of copycats. However, the limitation of copycats is that they easily get lost in the shadows once the real thing comes on stage.

A great purpose statement must be clear on the points of departure from the competition even in the same industry or sector.

This is done by emphasizing the exclusive and distinctive benefits that your customers shall reap courtesy of your service and product offering. You could also consider emphasizing the unique approach your business employs to deliver the desired outcome intended for the customers.

Take the examples of Kenya Commercial Bank Group and Equity Group Holdings, both leading brands in the banking industry in East and Central Africa.

KCB's purpose statement:

Simplifying your world to enable your progress. [9]

Equity Group Holding's purpose statement:

Transforming Lives, giving dignity and expanding opportunities for wealth creation. [7]

Even though both are in the Banking industry, their focus and what they aim to achieve are very distinct from each other. Whereas KCB's focus is to simplify their customers' lives to help them make progress through the use of technology and innovative products, Equity's focus is about transformation of lives, giving dignity and wealth creation opportunities to its customers by providing revolutionary and non-traditional banking and other related products targeting the unbanked and the under banked segments of the populations.

Two behemoth banking conglomerates with two different and distinct purposes and both have astounding success in their different target markets.

e) It must have creative tension

A powerful purpose statement is one that elicits creative tension among those charged with its execution. It should clearly arouse a strong desire for its pursuit by making its achievement a remarkable possibility but which nonetheless requires some dedicated work.

A great purpose statement should call for a continuous innovation and a growth mindset that puts the company on a path of always striving but never truly arriving.

Take the example of the purpose statement of Safaricom Ltd (Kenya):

> *"Our goal is for our products and services to transform lives and contribute to sustainable living throughout Kenya"*[10]

The goal of transforming lives is always a moving target; the more you do the more the possibilities of better quality and higher standards come to the fore. This puts the company on a never ending path of continuous innovation and creativity.

Safaricom's fidelity to this cause has had a tremendous positive impact on people's lives and livelihoods in Kenya besides permanently disrupting the telecommunications industry in the country.

f) Make it both brief and memorable

Lastly, a purpose statement is more impactful if it is brief and memorable. Every staff member should know it off head word for word without paraphrasing the same.

This greatly influences the day-to-day decisions and the conduct of the team members, as the purpose gradually becomes the defining standard for staff behavior and demeanor.

Let's take two examples:

1. *"To live and deliver WOW "*[11]

That's the purpose statement of Zappos.com—a leading US Based online shoe and clothing retailer. Those five words convey the customer-centric business philosophy and Zappos' obsession to turn every client interaction with the brand at every touch point to a joyous and delightful experience.

Zappos employees know the purpose statement by heart and relentlessly strive to deliver the same; the customers on the other hand also expect the WOW experience at every touch when interacting with Zappos and that's what they always get.

The phenomenal rise of Zappos.com is adequate testimony to the efficacy of this terse purpose statement.

2. *"Refresh the World. Make a difference"*

That's the purpose statement of the giant soft-drink manufacturer, The Coca-Cola Company.

So brief and memorable yet so full of meaning; it also clearly resonates very well with Coca-Cola employees, its partners and consumers.

It should not come as a surprise that Coca-Cola Company products have reached every part of the globe and have become part and parcel of every large celebration anywhere in the world for several decades now.

◆ ◆ ◆

Have A Relook At Your Purpose Statement

As we come to the end of this chapter, we advise that it is time to have a fresh look at your business purpose statement if you already have one in place, and see how relevant it is in driving your business. You need to check whether it is clearly communicating your WHY of doing business!

You also need to evaluate your purpose statement based on these key parameters discussed above:

- *Is it customer-centric?*

- *Is it inspiring?*

- *Is it differentiated?*

- *Does it elicit creative tension?*

- *It is brief and memorable?*

Either way, you can still take cues from the industry titans and their grand examples above, and begin your journey of building a real impactful business brand that will give you super returns irrespective of the state of the economy and prevailing cut-throat competition.

Start by having a clear and compelling purpose statement.

We can now move on to the next secret of the super brands, the next pillar that underpins their great success.

Turn with us to the next Chapter.

Reflection Questions

1) How clear and unequivocal is your brand's purpose? Is it known to all the relevant stakeholders?

2) What specific desired outcomes do your customers get by consuming your business products?

3) How aligned and relevant is your current product offering in

meeting the above desired outcome?

CHAPTER TWO: PHILOSOPHY

Making use of inspiring and empowering business philosophies

"Your income is directly related to your philosophy not the economy"

~JIM ROHN

In this chapter, we shall explore the second pillar or secret of the super brands, the power of business philosophies. More specifically *it is making use of inspiring and empowering business philosophies.*

Once you are clear on the purpose of your business, the next step is to determine how to pursue it. This is where the use of liberating and empowering business philosophies to both rally your team to a common cause and to inspire productivity comes in.

It has been shown that pursuit of every worthy cause requires a growth mindset coupled with a strong staying power capable of overcoming every inevitable obstacle and temporary upsets on the way. Growth mindset is a product of embracing empowering and liberating philosophies.

A super brand typically pursues its brand's purpose by employing strategic business philosophies designed to steer the company to achieve its mission and vision.

Empowering business philosophies are both foundational and instrumental for building powerful industrious cultures of excellence within corporations. These philosophies essentially become the focal points for rallying teams towards common objectives.

From time immemorial, great leaders have understood the hidden power of curated philosophies in influencing corporate cultures and rallying people towards desired outcomes. Witty industry captains have used similar weapons to conquer new territories and dominate markets, while effectively vanquishing competition in the process.

Philosophies And Business Success:

Successful business brands are anchored on time tested business philosophies that engage the hearts and minds of the employees on the one hand, while captivating the imaginations and adoration of the target customers to the point of enlisting their enthusiastic patronage on the other hand.

These unique inspiring and empowering business philosophies serve as the steering wheel that guides leading businesses in both their day-to-day operations and long term strategies, effectively creating corporate cultures of excellence that enables the meticulous execution of winning business strategies.

The end result of the steadfast and concerted execution of the ground breaking business ideas and winning strategies inevitably ushers these brands to positions of market dominance.

To gather and unify their tribe of ardent believers and armies of enthusiastic supporters, leading brands normally deploy appealing ideologies in action that both promises and delivers a sense of camaraderie and accomplishment to those tasked with the execution of the brand's purpose on the one hand while ensuring a thriving business culture and approach that is endearing to the customers on the other hand.

Furthermore, to build a great business brand, the desired outcome of pursuing these corporate purposes must of necessity yield true value to the customers.

In other words, to be truly phenomenal, a business approach must of necessity be unique, inspiring and engaging to those tasked with delivering the desired outcome; equally the business approach must be both alluring and resonating well with the target customers.

As already noted, to enable the core purpose of the brand to come alive, the leadership of these super brands intentionally and relentlessly deploys empowering business philosophies capable of rallying the teams towards the desired outcomes.

Successful use of these uplifting business philosophies inevitably results into employees' ownership of the business processes and their taking of responsibility for the outcome of the same. Such a situation not only presents a momentous and invaluable corporate treasure to any business, but it is also an automatic game changer for the company involved.

What Then Is Business Philosophy?

It is not in the scope of this book to give academic definition of philosophy. We therefore offer our unreserved apologies to scholars and students of philosophy who may be disappointed by our working definition of philosophy as far as business management is concerned.

In this book,we define business philosophy as:

> *An ideal that the company leadership espouses for the company members to operate and live by.*

We can also describe a business philosophy as the espoused collective mindset through which a company pursues its purpose.

All the super brands have deliberately curated and deeply ingrained certain winning philosophies within their entire fabric that guide their business operations in general and their day-to-day interactions with their customers in particular. These corporate philosophies serve as the mantras that the members of the company live and operate by.

The impact of corporate philosophies in business:

The monumental impact of empowering business philosophies on the brand's performance and positioning is only beginning to be truly appreciated by thought leaders and industry captains.

To start with, the business philosophies typically shape the company's world outlook and how their members view their relationship with and contribution to the world.

Secondly, these espoused ideals are designed to influence and shape the corporate culture. Corporate culture in turn serves as the habitat within which the company strategies either thrive or die.

Thirdly, both the long-term and short-term business objectives of companies are strategically guided and inadvertently impacted by the adopted philosophies. This is because the corporate philosophies serve as the engine oil that keeps the company engine running smoothly. To be effective therefore, the corporate philosophies adopted must reinforce and be aligned with the brand's purpose.

Moreover, adopting liberating and uplifting brand philosophies inevitably results into enhanced staff productivity and the accompanying meteoric business growth. On the other hand, lack of clear corporate ideologies or having dull and limiting ones effectively choke staff productivity and thereby impeding the company growth.

It therefore follows that adopting empowering business philosophies essentially create powerful corporate cultures of excellence conducive for peak performance and superb cost management. This state of affairs results into super profitability of the company on a sustainable basis.

◆ ◆ ◆

Business Philosophies And The Company Fabric

It is not enough for a brand just to have powerful philosophies, they must of necessity be embraced and practiced by all the members of the organization in order to truly harness their power and realize their impact.

> *The entire fabric of the company must be thoroughly permeated by these philosophies if they are to achieve their intended purpose for the brand.*

In other words, both the rank and file and the entire leadership of the company essentially must live by the values espoused by the company philosophies.

To fully exploit the power of corporate philosophies, their adoption must go beyond the slogans either merely pasted on office walls or written on the company websites, to be embraced in the hearts and minds of all the company members as the right and expected way to do things.

This is one secret of the leading brands that has enabled them to register phenomenal growth and astounding success.

For example, Huawei's central philosophy of *customer centricity* is not just a slogan but the norm of business operations for both Huawei's leadership and staff. This reality is highlighted in these words from the founder Ren Zhengfei:

> *Serving our customers is the only reason why Huawei exists. This should be something that our people believe in their hearts and live out in their actions. It cannot be merely a slogan.*[1]

The Three Classes Of Business Philosophies

Business philosophies are expressed in three main ways. And incidentally, every super brand works with a combination of these classes of business philosophies in one form or another, to achieve their broad objectives.

The three classes are:

- *Operational business philosophies*
- *Mission-critical core values*
- *Captivating and memorable brand slogans*

We shall explore them hereunder:

a) Operational Business Philosophies

Operational business philosophies are the foundational schools of thoughts or the bedrock upon which the company strategies, policies and procedures are anchored.

They can also be described as the spirit of the culture within the company.

Operational business philosophies are so central to the success or failure of the business to be left to chance.

It should be noted that the other two categories of business philosophies—*the core values* and *the brand slogans,* only serve to reinforce and support the underlying operational philosophies.

These operational business philosophies are either formally written down or in some instances remains informal. It is however worth noting that all leading brands have operational business philosophies that are formally written down and properly articulated to all staff.

Let's now look at three examples of brands that have successfully applied operational business philosophies and reaped massive benefits as a result thereof.

1. Samsung Group

This South Korean technology giant continues to dominate the electronics and smart devices market and has remained the undisputed leader, with its cutting-edge inventions and superior products.

The company was ranked in the 5th position among the global most valuable brands by the *Brand Finance Top 500 Brands* for two consecutive years (2019 and 2020) owing to its relentless devotion to superior quality products and superior customer service.

This sterling performance by Samsung Group has been made possible because of its relentless fidelity to the group's business philosophy *"to devote its talent and technology to creating superior products and services that contribute to a better global society"*[2]

This philosophy is reflected in everything that Samsung brand is associated with.

Of importance to note is that Samsung Group continuously engages in extensive research in technology and customers' needs to not only get an in-depth understanding of their customers' needs and preferences but also to remain a pacesetter and influencer of technological advancement.

This trend is evidenced by the lead role Samsung Inc. is currently playing in the development and rollout of 5G mobile phones and networks. As of November 2019, Samsung group controlled 54% of the global 5G market.[3]

2. *Huawei Technologies Co. Ltd*

Huawei Company, the Chinese global leader in ICT infrastructure and smart devices manufacturing has recently burst into the limelight and was ranked at position 10 by *Brand Finance* among 500 Global brands in 2020[4], effectively beating many well established brands.

The meteoric rise of this brand has been made possible owing to its singular commitment to twin brand philosophies of '*Customer-Centricity*' and '*Relentless Pursuit of Innovation in an Open Ecosystem*' in its quest *to expand the benefits of technology to everyone, everywhere.*[5]

Huawei Company has invested heavily in research and product development to not only understand their customers' needs and create customized technology solutions for the same but also to aid the company in anticipating and shaping the future trends.

Whereas many companies talk of being customer-focused without any accompanying tangible policies and actions, under the leadership of its founder and CEO Ren Zhengfei, Huawei company operates on a policy of '*might from a small hole*'[6] by which the company leadership spares no resources in their unwavering commitment to achieve their sharply defined purpose of enriching lives through the benefits of technology.

Just like water that can cut through steel plates once highly pressurized through a small opening, Huawei firmly believes that through its continued commitment of resources to research and development in pursuit of this purpose, it can consistently improve.

Huawei company's impressive performance results and the meteoric rise in the global technology industry have vindicated the efficacy of the above policy of massive resource deployment in product research and development.

3. Tesla Inc.

Tesla Inc. (formerly Tesla Motors Inc.) under the leadership of Elon Musk is arguably the world's fastest growing brand in terms of value, according to *Brand Finance Global 500 Brands 2020 report.* [7]

In pursuit of its purpose *'to accelerate the planet's transition to sustainable energy'*[8], the company rides on the twin business philosophies of *'lack of bureaucracy'* and *'adherence to first principles method'*[9] to race ahead of the competition.

The philosophy of *First Principles Method* or first principles thinking requires someone to dig deeper and deeper until one is left with only the foundational truths of the situation. This thinking has helped Tesla Inc. to inexpensively develop state-of-the-art solar powered inventions and electric cars thus debunking the myth that every ground-breaking invention must cost an arm and a leg.

On the philosophy of *Lack of bureaucracy* at Tesla Inc., Elon Musk has taken the lead to remove red tape and all communications barriers within the entire fabric of the company, so as to ensure faster communication flow and sharing of great ideas within Tesla Inc.

In a famed e-mail communication from the CEO Elon Musk to all Tesla Inc. employees, Musk laid bare his demands for open communication and true collaboration throughout Tesla and for the benefit of Tesla.

Here are some excerpts of the referenced e-mail:

"Anyone at Tesla can, and should email/talk to anyone else according to what they think is the fastest way to solve a problem for the benefit of the whole company. You can talk to your manager's manager without his permission, you can talk directly to a VP in another dept, you can talk to me, you can talk to anyone without anyone else's permission…

…we are all in the same boat. Always view yourself as working for the good of the company and never your dept." [10]

Such a communication is a clear directive from the chief executive for the company members to steer clear of any bureaucracies while at the same time encouraging spontaneity and faster sharing of ideas and information among the employees without regard to ranks, titles and departments.

Indeed the processes and product innovations at Tesla Inc. can authoritatively be credited to the successful application of the twin philosophies of ***First Principles Method*** and ***lack of bureaucracy*** at Tesla.

Elon Musk is a leader who has earned his respect and right to speak on these matters. Musk's directives have had a huge positive impact on the company's culture and business operations. And Tesla Inc. has the results to show for it.

Musk's leadership and business approach has undoubtedly steered Tesla Inc. to the position of global dominance, besides creating enormous shareholder value in the process.

The three examples above aptly illustrate the power of operational business philosophies when successfully implemented.

We shall now look at the second aspect of business philosophies.

b) Mission-critical Core Values

The second aspect of the corporate philosophies is reflected in mission-critical core values.

Far from the generic core values lacking contextual meaning that are prevalent in most average companies, leading business brands only work with mission-critical core values that aid their continued creativity and productivity.

Moreover, these mission critical core values aid in the excellent service delivery to the customers, with added emphasis on the brand's uniqueness in the market.

The core values adopted by all leading brands address only three key aspects of their business operations:

- *The key focus area which is customer satisfaction (customer-centricity)*

- *The means of delivering the customer satisfaction (operational excellence) and*

- *The spirit of delivering the service excellence (integrity).*

It should be noted that these core values have as many names or descriptions as the number of companies that are involved.

We shall explore each of these mission-critical core values below:

i. <u>Customer-centricity</u>

This is the first core value of all the super brands. It is the value that reflects the brand's obsession with their customers' interests in both attitude and actions.

Some companies call it *'customers first'* while other brands call it *'customer obsession'*

> *To stay ahead of the game, a brand must stay focused on what truly matters: that is to offer superior customer experience.*

All the brand processes and strategies of the super brands are designed to give the customers the best experience at every touch point with the particular brands. From market research and product development, to product design, sales and marketing and after sale service, it is all about customers.

These companies truly believe and show by their actions that *'the customer is the king'*. To these super brands, this phrase is not an empty mantra.

Achieving sustainable super profitability is the natural outgrowth of serving an ever increasing pool of satisfied and loyal customers who not only increase their average spending on your company products but also refer their friends and other acquaintances to your business.

When a brand solely focuses on goals that matter, it definitely wins in the war of customer acquisition and retention; and in the process, the brand makes handsome profits.

Let's look at three examples to drive this point home:

a) *Amazon's philosophy of customer obsession rather than competitor focus*

One of the four principles of Amazon Inc. that has propelled the brand to the position of global dominance is *Customer obsession rather than competitor focus.*[11] This is in line with Amazon's purpose *'to be the Earth's most customer centric company'*

As a core value, this principle focuses Amazon as a company to steer clear of all the distractions of trying to match or outdo every competitor action but instead remain a pacesetter in the online retail industry, championing customers' best interests.

Amazon has clearly mastered the wisdom of the sages of old: *the wisdom of focusing on continuous self-improvement in order to increase your earning capacity.*

The late American industrialist and business magnate Henry Ford said that:

> *"The competitor to be feared is the one who never bothers about you at all, but goes on making his own business better all the time."*

And Amazon Company has the excellent results to show for this relentless pursuit of self-improvement instead of focusing on every competitor action. The company has not only continued to dominate the online retail industry as the most profitable and valuable brand but it has effectively attained the industry pacesetter status to boot.

b) Huawei's philosophy of customer centricity

The Chinese technology behemoth, Huawei Company has perfected the use of customer-centricity both as an operational business philosophy and as a core value to their great advantage.

Ren Zhengfei, Huawei's founder and CEO describes their commitment to customer-centricity as follows:

> *Huawei doesn't aim to maximize the interests of its shareholders or employees. Huawei only exists to serve its customers. This is why Huawei has and will continue to succeed.* [12]

Ren further declares succinctly in response to a question on Huawei culture as follows:

> *Our culture is very simple: staying customer-centric and inspiring dedication.* [13]

Customer-centricity is more than a phrase at Huawei; on the contrary, it is the defining attribute that has permeated every decision, strategy and action of Huawei employees and the leadership team.

c) Zappos commitment to deliver WOW to its customers
Giant US based online shoes and clothing retailer Zappos.com is the undisputed leader in matters customer-centricity. The first on the list of its core values is to *"deliver WOW through service"*.[14]

This core value effectively captures the spirit of customer obsession with which Zappos approaches all its product and service offering. Zappos.com has succeeded to transform client interactions with the brand at every touch point into a joyous and exciting experience.

As a result Zappos.com has registered a phenomenal growth to become dominant in its industry, propelled primarily by an army of satisfied evangelical customers who have undoubtedly tasted and appreciated the WOW experience from Zappos.

ii. <u>Operational Excellence</u>

The second core value of the super brands addresses the means by which the superior customer experience is delivered.

The spirit of operational excellence demands that the core processes are streamlined and supported to give the best experiences to the customers; and that teams and individual employees work together in the spirit of co-operation and harmony for the benefit of the brand.

Super brands usually go to great lengths to streamline their core processes to remove any inbuilt bureaucracies and bottlenecks in the service delivery. In other words, super brands typically and progressively align their systems to enhance products' quality and improve service standards.

Continuous system audit to align processes and operations is a common feature in all leading companies in every industry. Every procedure that is deemed to have outlived its usefulness is quickly detected and removed. At the same time, new effective and better techniques of doing business operations are routinely adopted.

Moreover, quality checks are embedded in the production and service delivery systems to ensure that customers get nothing but the best in terms of products and services quality.

It is important to note that these brands always ensure that they hire competent and qualified staff in all the key roles within the establishment. Their employees are further exposed to very rigorous and continuous on the job trainings and refresher courses to keep them abreast with service delivery expectations of excellence at all times. (NB: You can read more on this in Chapter three of this book)

Furthermore, clear service charters which are known by both the employees and the customers, are made use of to ensure that both groups are on the same page as far as service delivery expectations is concerned. This is further reinforced with instituted self-escalating compliance monitoring systems.

Hereunder we shall look at the core value of operational excellence in action within a super brand:

The example of Safaricom Ltd

Safaricom ltd is the leading telecommunications company in East Africa and is by far the most profitable brand among all listed companies on the Nairobi Stock Exchange (NSE).

With a total of **35.6 million** active customers, representing **64.5%** of mobile phone subscribers in Kenya as at March 2020, Safaricom ltd effectively dominates the Kenyan mobile telephone market.[15]

For a company which has only been operational since year 2000, its meteoric rise is a case worth studying.

To start with, Safaricom ltd has refined and simplified its business approach by reducing its strategic objectives to just three[16]:

    a) *Customer first*

b) *Relevant products*

c) *Operational excellence*

It is very clear from this refined business approach that Safaricom Ltd truly focuses only on what matters in as far as building a super brand is concerned.

Our focus in this section is to explore how Safaricom ltd has used operational excellence to steer ahead of the competition and become a great brand.

Safaricom ltd has embraced the spirit of operational excellence in all its business dealings within and without the company. In its released sustainability report 2016, the company describes operational excellence as follows:

> *Operational excellence requires us to assess every aspect of the business from the perspective of how well it is serving the customer and helping to deliver quality experiences to them.*[17]

Safaricom ltd uses the principle of operational excellence to streamline all its internal processes and to keep production costs within projected and acceptable levels.

In particular, the company meticulously applies operational excellence in such processes as:

- *Design of new relevant products*

- *Faster products delivery to the market*

- *Continuous technologically support of its products*

As a result of this business approach, Safaricom ltd has been able to develop relevant, exciting and tailored products that reverberate well with its various market segments. This has enabled the company to register more profitable sales every successive year to the point of achieving and maintaining the position of market dominance.

iii.   <u>Integrity</u>

This is the third core value cutting across all the super brands.

Some companies use the word *honesty;* others use the words *fairness, reliability, openness, trustworthiness* or any other such noun. The implication is the same.

Integrity is the virtue of being true to self, true to your customers and to your partners and remaining upright in all ones dealings, financial or otherwise. It is about uprightness of character or action.

Every great brand is built on the cornerstone of integrity. Without integrity a business can neither stand the test of time nor go very far, as the foundations would sooner or later prove faulty and the house will tumble with a bang.

Customers typically trust brands that have demonstrated high integrity in their dealings; brands whose products and services give true value for money spent on acquiring the same. (NB: You can read more about products and services in chapter Five (5) of this book).

In every industry, there are companies whose products have become synonymous with superior quality. Such brands have earned the trust of the consumers because of their consistent great quality merchandise and superior services.

Such highly regarded companies even have the leeway to charge premium prices if they so wished; moreover, they also do not have to overly spend on marketing and advertising as their products already have positive public reviews and the priceless word of mouth advertisement from their armies of satisfied evangelical customers.

The use of short-cuts or inferior materials in production may appear a *'smart move'* in the short-term as it *'saves'* costs and therefore *'maximizes profits'* but in the end it is both self-defeating and ultimately suicidal. Sooner or later, it becomes apparent that the company in question is a cheat, and the logical consequence of such unpleasant discoveries is the inevitable fall of the respective brand as the market *'sorts them out'*; in the process such a brand incurs serious reputational damage that often proves both costly and ruinous.

Many business conglomerates some of whom were considered too big to fail have been swept by the wayside when it became apparent that the brands were either insincere in some of their dealings or were engaged in active cover ups of costly blunders.

It should be noted that the business world is very intolerant to revelations of dishonesty and cover-ups of unfair deals by corporations. Such revelations more often than not prove to be these companies' *waterloo*.

Integrity as a virtue and a core value is therefore non-negotiable for any brand seeking to make headway in the market and win the loyalty and continued patronage of customers.

When we act with integrity, we find it easy to own up our mistakes and take responsibility for correcting the same.

Integrity also ensures that we do the right thing even when it is not convenient for us. Subsequently, we honor our words to our customers even when it is no longer expedient to do so.

In the process we earn the trust of our customers who find in us reliable and dependable partners worthy of their continued patronage.

Let's take one example of a super brand riding on the virtue of integrity to steer its growth and super profitability hereunder:

The example of Huawei Company
We have already mentioned the phenomenal growth of Huawei Company and its debut into the list of the top ten most valuable companies, in the *Brand Finance Top 500 year 2020 report*.

The Chinese technology behemoth has earned its place on the table of the movers and shakers of the new technology-driven world in part due to its relentless fidelity to the virtue of integrity.

Originally a *B2B* company, Huawei earned the trust of its corporate customers owing to its continued supply of high quality products and world class service anchored on the cornerstone of integrity.

Huawei Company founder Ren Zhengfei describes the centrality of integrity at Huawei as follows:

> *"The essence of Huawei's culture can be described with one word: integrity.*[18]

Weiwei Huang in his book *Built on value: The Huawei Philosophy of Finance and Management* captures the place of integrity in all the operations and dealings of Huawei from Ren Zhengfei's report as follows:

> *Huawei is not solely focused on profits. We aim for long-term development. We always act with integrity in regards to our customer engagement, operations, and corporate development. It is integrity that helps us earn customer satisfaction, trust, and loyalty. By not overly focusing on profits, we can spend more of our energy on diligently pursuing long-term development, rather than on hype or speculation.*[19]

And Huawei's results buttresses a fundamental but unconventional understanding that profitability is a natural by-product of focusing on the goals that matter such as delivering customer satisfaction through superior quality products offering and service excellence, rather than focusing on hype and speculation.

Let's now explore the third category of the business philosophies.

c) Captivating and memorable brand slogans

The third aspect of corporate philosophies is in the use of corporate slogans.

Super brands typically condense the essence of their business philosophies into memorable and revolutionizing corporate slogans that capture the spirit of their brand's purpose.

These corporate slogans thereafter become part and parcel of the brand identity.

Brands use these corporate slogans to unequivocally communicate the brand promise to the employees, the customers and other stakeholders.

The corporate slogans hugely impact and shape the internal cultures of the companies; their impact on the employees' morale when duly reinforced with the right policies and procedures is humongous.

Moreover, a great corporate slogan enables the customers to visualize the company products and to think favorably about the company.

When these slogans are appropriately crafted to resonate well with the target consumers, they inevitably propel the various brands to positions of market dominance.

It has been established that great slogans do inspire lots of emotional connection with a brand while catchy slogans make brands more recognizable and memorable.

Take the examples of Huawei's slogan *"Make it Possible"* and Walmart's *"Save Money, Live Better"* which have not only captured the imaginations of millions of people who have become ardent patrons of the respective brands but also hugely impacted the *modus operandi* of the same brands. The respective company's policies, procedures, strategies and core values all reflect the spirit of these slogans.

Let's discuss two more examples:

1. *"The Best or Nothing." – Mercedes Benz*

The leading German Automobile manufacturer Mercedes-Benz has successfully internalized its brand slogan of *"The Best or Nothing"* and infused the same into everything the company does; all its products and services quality is a living testimony of the reality of this ideology.

This simple four word phrase represents the essence of what Mercedes-Benz Company stands for as a brand. It communicates their commitment to be the best in every aspect of Automobile manufacturing, right from innovation, to design, to performance and safety.

While staying true to the spirit of *the best or nothing* ideology, Mercedes-Benz has endeavored to manufacture state-of-the-art automobile machines that deliver fashion statement, style, high quality and safety, all in one package.

This relentless pursuit of excellence has seen Mercedes-Benz continue to dominate global automobile industry for decades now.

According to Brand Finance Global 500—2020 report, Mercedes-Benz was ranked at position 10 among the most valuable global brands in 2020, up from position 15 in the year 2019. [20]

2. *"Work hard. Have Fun. Make History"—Amazon Inc.*

Amazon Inc. has dominated the list of Top 500 Global Brands for three years in a row, since 2018 according to Brand Finance rankings. This performance is attributed to among other things, the spirit of Amazon's corporate slogan: *"Work hard. Have Fun. Make History"*[21]

This slogan signifies the brand's ideology to inculcate aspiration for creativity and innovation for the Amazon team, while they enjoy the work in the process, but which nonetheless still requires the employees to pull their weight.

A call to work hard and have fun in the process while cognizant of the fact that your effort however mundane is playing a vital role in making world history, has been a very ingenious way to rally the Amazon team to give their best effort in the pursuit of Amazon's purpose, and the result has been a definite shot at greatness.

Below is a list of additional examples of inspiring corporate slogans of some brands that have had a great impact on the brands' performances in their own industries:

- *Just do it* (Nike)

- *Do what you can't* (Samsung Inc.)

- *New world, New Thinking* (Lenovo)

- *Think Different* (Apple Inc.)
- *It's finger lickin' good* (KFC)
- *Open Happiness* (Coca-Cola)
- *I'm lovin' it* (McDonald's)
- *Your listening, Caring Partner* (Equity Group Holdings)

You probably already identify with these slogans even without mentioning the various brands they represent. The brands above are hugely popular with the public besides being highly esteemed by their customers.

Leading brands revise their corporate slogans overtime.

Please also note that super brands normally revise their corporate slogans overtime to reflect the changing phases of their business growth. This is done to best capture the spirit of the company growth strategies and corporate focus at any particular period.

A good example is the Samsung Group which has modified its corporate slogan overtime. From its business slogan of *"Everyone is Invited"* of the years 1999-2002 to the current slogan of *"Do What You Can't"* (2017-present), Samsung Group has changed its corporate slogan at least six times.

Rules For Creating Corporate Philosophies

To start with, it is worth mentioning that that every company either wittingly or unwittingly operates on a set of philosophies which ultimately define the company's prevailing culture. Even your own business has or will operate under certain philosophies by default or by design. So why not take the lead and influence the kind of philosophies that will propel your brand to success and greatness?

When a company is still under the leadership of its founders, it is pretty easy to influence the corporate philosophies as they will majorly be the ideals of the founders. However when the business has grown and is under new leadership team either hired from without or promoted from within, it behooves the leadership to craft and help ingrain uplifting and empowering business philosophies to permeate the entire fabric of the company.

Either way it still takes tact and dexterity on the part of leadership to create and enforce the espoused ideologies.

All said and done, how then do you craft appropriate corporate philosophies for your own company?

In this section we shall show you how you too can craft your own powerful business philosophies and harness their immense potential thereof to your brand's great advantage.

The following are the fundamental rules for crafting inspiring and empowering corporate philosophies:

- *They must be aligned with the brand's purpose*

- *They must be appealing*

- *They must be pithy and forceful*

- *They must be compelling*
- *They must be audacious*

We shall explore these rules hereunder:

a) *They must be aligned with the brand's purpose.*

Corporate philosophies are primarily designed to drive the achievement of the brand's purpose. They must therefore be in tandem and properly aligned with the company purpose. In other words, the import of each business philosophy adopted by the company must be to further the cause of the brand.

Furthermore, corporate philosophies should be crafted in such a way that they conjure up positive imaginations associated with the consumption of the company's products and services.

The target consumers should be able to make subtle connections between these corporate philosophies and the brands that they represent.

We shall look at two examples to illustrate this point:

i. <u>*'Open Happiness'*—The Coca-Cola Company</u>

The giant soft drinks manufacturer—The Coca-Cola Company's corporate slogan of *'Open Happiness'* is truly in line with its core purpose to *'Refresh the world and Make a difference.'*

Coca-Cola has successfully made inroads in the entire globe and become part and parcel of every major celebration the world over, by subtly associating the consumption of its products with happiness or any kind of celebrations.

It would interest you to note also that all the commercial adverts by the Coca-Cola Company are associated with joyous celebrations and camaraderie among the consumers. The individuals depicted in the adverts as consuming the soft drinks are always in a jolly mood regardless of their age, gender, race or occupation hence the fitting corporate slogan of *Open Happiness.*

ii.   <u>*'It's finger lickin' good'*—KFC</u>

KFC's *'It's finger lickin' good'* slogan augurs well with its mouth-watering fried chiecken. The catchy phrase conjures up images of something mouthwatering and yummy such as fried chicken.

When you hear or see this slogan, you immediately connect it with something sweet and delicious and that is the exact intention of KFC—to have its customers to associate yummy and delicious fried chicken with KFC.

b) *They must be appealing*

Corporate philosophies are more effective if they are attractive, engaging and likeable. They must appeal to people's hearts and minds and draw them to the brand's cause.

Two examples will serve to illustrate this point:

i.   <u>Lenovo's corporate slogan of *'New world, New Thinking'*</u>

The slogan both challenges and conditions the company personnel to stretch their imaginations and invent cutting-edge revolutionary products; the company customers are equally hyped to expect great and unconventional products from Lenovo.

Even more importantly, Lenovo's smart devices are effectively associated with new thinking in a new technology driven world courtesy of this slogan. The use of this company's products is touted to imply advancement on the part of the consumers and therefore to be desired as valuable devices.

> ii.   <u>Walmart's *'Save money. Live better'* corporate slogan.</u>

The US based retail giant has successfully pursued its corporate purpose *"to save people money so they can live better"* judging by its huge popularity in the market and dominance in the global traditional retail space to boot.

The retailer condensed its purpose essence to a simple yet appealing corporate slogan which has become synonymous with the brand—*Save money. Live better.*

Walmart Inc. relentlessly works to avail a variety of retail merchandise in the most cost effective and convenient ways to the reach of millions of its customers, so that their budget conscious customers can get good value for their money without the risk of purchasing inferior quality products.

This has been made possible by the multiple Walmart stores across the globe including its online e-commerce platform *Walmart.com*

This philosophy has resonated very well with the budget-conscious customers who happen to be the majority in the retail consumers segment; Walmart stores' records of millions of visits by shoppers in its stores and hypermarkets on a weekly basis is a testimony of the efficacy of this appealing philosophy.

And who would not mind saving their hard earned income and still get quality merchandise at great bargains!

c) *They must be pithy and forceful*

Winning corporate philosophies are brief, concise and sharp

to make them memorable. Long phrases or wordy sentences will not do for great philosophies.

Check all the corporate slogans and operational business philosophies you can easily remember and associate with any brand, you will note that they are brief and concise.

Examples include:

- Customer-centricity (Huawei Technologies Co. Ltd)
- New World. New Thinking (Lenovo)
- The Best or Nothing (Mercedes-Benz)

d) *They must be compelling*

Winning ideologies are those that are persuasive, captivating and exciting, and therefore capable of moving people to action. It should of necessity present a clarion call for a desired cause of action.

Huawei's *"Make it possible"* and Nike's *'Just do it'* slogans best illustrate this.

e) *They must be audacious*

Lastly great ideologies are bold and audacious and their pursuit presents an element of risk.

Great brands are built on philosophies and goals whose pursuit has a real possibility of failure. This forces the companies to either build more capacity or to work around the clock to find a way out.

The thrill in the purpose's achievements is more pronounced due to the risk of failure that is inherent in the process.

Two examples will serve to illustrate this point:

i.   Mercedes Benz slogan of *'The best or nothing'* is very daring and undoubtedly bold. The company is staking its reputation on being the best on anything automobile; this not only stretches the creativity and imagination of the company staff, but with every passing day, there is a real risk that their product quality might not be the best in the market owing to the possibility of new competitors' superior innovations.

ii.   The giant technology company Samsung's Group slogan of '*Do What You Can't*' is a clear call to break through every barrier and shatter every limitation real or imagined in its endeavor to create superior products and services that contribute to a better global society.

Consequently, Samsung Group has set a high value on its employees and technologies.[22]

Samsung Group relentlessly pursues product research and innovations to find ways to deliver inventions that were previously imagined to be impossible.

This philosophy continuously presents creative tension to Samsung as each new milestone is achieved and new possibilities of further innovations come to the fore to be pursued.

It is little wonder therefore that Samsung Group is currently playing a leading role in 5G network infrastructure rollouts and smart devices production in the world today.

How To Enforce The Corporate Philosophies

As we come to the end of this chapter, we will close by giving you tips on how to enforce the corporate philosophies in order to reap their immense benefits.

Hereunder are some of the proven ways of enforcing corporate philosophies:

i.   *Make them public*

ii.   *The leadership must Lead from the front*

iii.   *Incorporate the corporate philosophies in the employee reward mechanism*

iv.   *Keep talking about them*

Let's now explore these points for better undertanding of the same below:

i.   Make them public

Corporate philosophies work best when they are made public. This move effectively raises public expectation and cajoles every employee to live by the espoused ideals.

By going public with your business philosophies, you are essentially subjecting yourself to higher accountability from constituencies outside of your company; the public effectively becomes the jury.

Going public is an open declaration to the world the information about who you are and what you stand for and inviting the world to judge you on those commitments. Such a commitment has incredible power to keep you on your toes.

You essentially become accountable to your customers, suppliers, and all other interested stakeholders. But the positive results from such a commitment are worth every effort.

ii.   The leadership must lead from the front

Leadership is about influence. To a great extent the underlying corporate philosophies in every organization is nothing more than the reflections of the ideals of the leader(s).

In this regard, corporate philosophies are only effective when they are demonstrated and truly exemplified by the leadership in their day-to-day actions and decisions. Anything short of this is merely cheap talk and therefore inconsequential.

For example, if the company operates on the philosophy of *customer-centricity*, it must be demonstrated by the leadership that the customers truly come first by how they respond to customer service issues. The rest of the employees will take note and behave accordingly.

This is because more often than not corporate culture is caught more than is taught.

iii.   Incorporate them in the employee reward mechanism

The fastest way to enforce corporate values is to incorporate them in the reward and compensation scheme. What gets measured gets done; equally what gets rewarded gets repeated.

Demonstrating the core values or the espoused ideals should form a portion of the staff appraisal scores as a company policy. Such virtues as team work, positive work attitude, respect for customers and colleagues etc. should be recognized and appropriately rewarded.

Staff promotions should be more or less a function of demonstrating the espoused company philosophies as much as it is about delivering the numbers.

It should be noted that for business sustainability, how the numbers are delivered should be considered to be equally important just like the numbers themselves.

iv. Keep talking about them

Use every available opportunity to speak about your corporate philosophies. Make these philosophies your regular song; keep talking about them in as many meetings with your team members as possible.

Make your corporate philosophies a mandatory part of the staff induction process. Incorporate them in your written communication with your employees as often as possible.

It has been observed that the grind of daily work and the accompanying pressures may make some people to lose track of these essentials, and this is not out of spite; it is therefore the responsibility of the leadership to keep their employees reminded about the company values and ideologies at all times.

Once you have put in place your corporate philosophies and are raring to use them in your business or organization, it is time to move on to the third secret of the super brands—the third ingredient responsible for their phenomenal brand success. Come with us to Chapter Three.

NB: We can clearly see that all super brands have perfected the use of this second pillar or second secret for business success: *The effective use of corporate philosophies*

Reflection Questions

1) Great leaders understand and harness the power of curated business philosophies to rally their teams towards common objectives and inspire great productivity. What is the current practice in your establishment?

2) How aligned and relevant are your business philosophies to your core brand purpose, and how deeply ingrained are they within your company fabric?

3) How can you ensure that your employees both own up the business processes and take responsibility for the outcome of the same?

CHAPTER THREE:
PEOPLE

*Working with competent quality
oriented inspired teams*

"People are not your most important asset. The right people are"

~JIM COLLINS

The next ingredient for building a super brand is the caliber of people you bring on board to be part of your team. The quality of the people a company works with makes all the difference.

The third secret of the Super brands is their preference and habit of *working with competent quality oriented inspired teams.*

Leading companies are very particular when it comes to the choice of their employees, because they understand one cardinal truth that *people are not the most important company asset, on the contrary the right people are.*

The success and sustainable growth of your business comes down to the kind of people you have on board.

Let's face it ladies and gentlemen:
- *Strong brands are built by teams that are committed to excellence.*
- *Cutting-edge innovations are done by persons who are driven by the desire to make a positive difference.*
- *Ground-breaking ideas that steer brands to greatness are born by ingenious people.*
- *Quality products are produced by quality-oriented people.*
- *Business strategies are meticulously implemented by inspired people.*
- *Superior customer service is offered by service excellence enthusiasts or aficionados.*

And the list goes on.

An organization can only be as great as the collective greatness of the people working in it especially the leadership team. ***When all is said and done, a brand only becomes great when it rides on the shoulders of great men and women.***

Super brands typically work with smart and tenacious people. This is an irrefutable fact that has been noted by thought leaders and leading business magnates alike.

Best-selling author and lecturer Jim Collins remarked that:

"Great vision without great people is irrelevant".

Leaders who have built great brands understand the power of working with gifted and talented people in their corporations. Whereas these leaders are seldom good at everything, their expertise is in the art of spotting top talent and conscripting the same into their teams.

These leaders not only recruit the right people but also build corporate cultures where top performers want to stay. They seek out and hire people who can burn the midnight oil while keeping the costs down, people who can deliver on the business promises, people who can stand strong under pressure and still show up enthusiastically to continue fighting another day after temporary upsets.

Great leaders know that it is this caliber of individuals who can collectively design, create and build the most successful businesses in any industry. They value-add and greatly enhance the vision bearers' dreams of building global revolutionary enterprises, and work tirelessly to make the dreams reality.

American entrepreneur and film producer, the late Walt Disney said that:

> *"You can dream, create, design and build the most wonderful place in the world…but it requires people to make the dream a reality"*

Great leaders surround themselves with smarter people.
Leading companies deliberately go to great lengths to hire and bring on board the best talent there is in the market and then pay them handsomely to retain their services. The best corporations in the world have mastered this practice to their great advantage.

> *The industry titans and all super performing companies in the world often pay the price to get the most gifted and skillful people on board instead of wasting their resources on mediocre and incompetent individuals who become leakages to their profits.*

Such brands understand that hiring the services of the best talents that bring real value to the company is not an expense but rather an investment.

◆ ◆ ◆

Super Achievers Are Smart And Tenacious People

To build a successful and sustainably profitable brand especially in these times of economic meltdowns, you need to have smart and tenacious people who are dedicated to excellence especially in your leadership team; you need people with enormous drive for winning, people who only draw their satisfaction from getting things done.

People who get things done come hell or high water are not only decisive on tough issues but they energize and work effectively through others. For such people, following through is their second nature.

When you have a team of such high achievers, your brand will inevitably deliver on its performance promises and build enormous value in the process thereof. Your company essentially becomes unstoppable.

Hereunder are a few quotes and observations from some of the world's leading entrepreneurs and business magnates on the impact of having the right talent on board:

i. Marc Benioff, the founder and chairman of Salesforce.com said the following on the significance of the hiring process:

"Acquiring the right talent is the most important key to growth. Hiring was – and still is – the most

important thing we do."

ii.   Microsoft Inc. Co-founder Bill Gates said that:

"The key for us, number one, has always been hiring very smart people."

iii.   American business magnate and Apple Co-founder, the late Steve Jobs while crediting their company success to the kind of people they hire and work with, said that:

"The secret to my success is that we've gone to exceptional lengths to hire the best people in the world."

iv.   Auren Hoffman, founder and CEO of Safegraph Company while commenting on the relationship that exists between a successful company and the right people, said that:

"Build teams of the smartest, nicest, get-stuff-done-ist people in the world. Then your company will be unstoppable"

v.   Business Coach and author Kevin J. Donaldson said that:

"Hiring the wrong people is the fastest way to

undermine a sustainable business."

Super Brands Hold Their People To Higher Performance Standards

The leadership of successful firms also tends to hold their people to higher standards of performance which invariably pushes them to give their best to the brand's cause; as a result deadlines are met and envisaged milestones are frequently achieved and celebrated.

Moreover, these companies not only give clear performance expectations to their employees, but they also create conducive and supportive work environments where such productivity can be achieved and surpassed. They thus create and maintain very high performance corporate cultures.

American business magnate and Co-founder of Apple Inc., the late Steve Jobs said that:

> *"I've learned over the years that, when you have really good people, you don't have to baby them. By expecting them to do great things, you can get them to do great things".*

When you have the right people who are committed to the brand's purpose, people who believe in your empowering brand philosophies, the word *'impossible'* effectively gets deleted from your company vocabulary. For such persons every problem becomes an opportunity to find new solutions; while every obstacle is viewed only as a temporary setback as new ingenious ways are quickly sought and discovered to address the same.

It is imperative to note that the corporate culture that a brand builds is pivotal to either the success or failure of the business.

Whereas a corporate culture is built by people, it eventually assumes a life of its own and thereafter either supports or actively vetoes the implementation of the company strategies.

Hire great people and give them room to perform their duties
The leaderships of super brands are particularly keen on the hiring process to ensure that they not only get those who can do the job with excellence but also those who will easily make the best cultural fit.

Great and confident leaders hire people who are smarter than them to run the core functions of the business, and then they get out of the way to enable the employees to do their work.

Former Ford Motors Company CEO Lee Iacocca credited their continued success in the automobile industry on the caliber of employees they brought on board and then gave the latitude to do their jobs. He said that:

> *"I hire people brighter than me and then I get out of their way"*

Mediocre and insecure leaders on the other hand hire people they are more comfortable working with, without the risk of been outshone. Unfortunately, this practice usually comes at a heavy price to the company that has to contend with increasing missed deadlines, burgeoning production costs and missed performance promises as a result of working with incompetent employees.

It has been noted that whereas having the right people greatly contributes to the brand's success, the surest path to ruin a great brand is to hire incompetent people.

Hiring wrong and incompetent staff especially in the leadership roles can bring down even the best placed corporations within a very short time.

That's why business Coach and author Kevin J. Donaldson noted that:

"Hiring the wrong people is the fastest way to undermine a sustainable business."

Until you address the issue of the caliber of people tasked with delivering your brand promise, you will only be marking time at best or actively regressing in your performance at worst as the best placed brands actively eat into your market share.

Who Is On Your Team?

When all has been said and done, we note that the caliber of people in an organization ultimately is a reflection of the organization's leadership. By default, the buck always stops at the corner office.

The best place to start addressing the people factor in your business is to do an honest assessment of your current team members.

As a leader, you need to ask yourself these pertinent questions:

  i. *Do I have the right people on the right roles?*
  ii. *Do I have the right mix of talents, gifts and expertise to drive my business to the desired level?*
  iii. *Does my team possess a 'whatever it takes' attitude necessary for accomplishing great things?*
  iv. *Does my leadership team have the emotional fortitude to follow through with their performance promises?*
  v. *Even more importantly, are my people just working for the paycheck or to advance the cause of the brand?*

Getting honest answers to the above reflective questions as unnerving as they may be, will lay a good foundation for addressing the all-important people factor in your business; subsequent follow through in addressing the identified gaps will set you on a course of transforming your business to a formidable brand. You essentially hold the golden key to unlock your business fortunes!

It has been proven time and again that the better the quality of the people a company hires and retains, the better the brand it shall build. Besides, whatever effort a company puts in finding the right people usually brings returns that cover the cost many times over.

It is also important to note that it usually proves both counter-productive and costly whenever a company choses not to invest in finding the right people to work with. Whatever costs the company *'saves'* by hiring average and mediocre employees quickly gets eroded as staff productivity plummets and production costs escalates in the hands of the incompetent work force.

Rules For Selecting The Right People

Whereas there are no *perfect* employees in the real sense of the word, there are certain valuable character traits or specific attributes that potential employees should possess in order to be considered for employment roles in growth oriented organizations. With little on-the-job training or skills sharpening, such employees will prove to be valuable assets to the respective companies as they pursue their broad objectives.

In this section, we shall discuss some rules for recruiting the right people.

There are many variables to consider when you are recruiting a winning team. We will however discuss the seven most important traits that you need to see in a potential employee in order to hire them:

- ✓ *Character*
- ✓ *Competence*
- ✓ *Positive energy*
- ✓ *Passion*
- ✓ *Cultural Fit*
- ✓ *Reliability*
- ✓ *Good communicator*

a) <u>Character</u>

Character should be at the top of your hiring checklist. Every new employee should have a moral standing beyond reproach.

> *Being of unquestionable character is the first non-negotiable attribute of a good hire.*

If you hire a person of integrity and sound work ethics, you can safely take care of teaching him any other nitty-gritties of the role. If on the other hand, the person lacks integrity but has all the other work qualifications or an impressive resume, hiring them is a time bomb that shall inevitably prove to be a costly blunder for the organization.

People without integrity will not only cause serious financial losses to the company, but they can also potentially cost the company disastrous reputational damages.

This is because defective character is like a pregnancy, it cannot be hidden for long; sooner or later it will show up.

It should be noted that no amount of training can produce good character. Equally, no amount of explaining the importance of good character can make it a practiced virtue in your company if it is not a personal attribute of the individual employees to begin with.

A brand starts to build integrity right from the people it hires. That's why the former president and CEO of Porsche, Peter Schutz advised that:

"Hire character. Train skill"

Always take time to conduct thorough background checks on your candidates before hiring them. Talk to their referees and ask pertinent questions on the values of these candidates to ascertain their *'true north'* status; to know how they relate with authority and peers, and how they manage resources under their care.

It is through these background checks that you can make your hiring decisions from a point of knowledge.

b) <u>Competence</u>

The second attribute is the competency of the candidate: their skills, gifts and talents that are necessary to get the job done. Competence also encompasses an individual's intelligence and business acumen.

A person's track record is very crucial in telling whether the individual has what it takes to get the job done.

Incompetence can easily be covered in periods of economic boom, when businesses are able to record good growth without the rigorous effort in strategizing, marketing and sales. Unfortunately those easy days are long gone and may not recur any time soon. ***Today, businesses are as successful as the level of competency and commitment of its people.***

In these times of great economic turbulence, job holders must possess the necessary expertise to successfully navigate both the market and industry related storms and still deliver on the performance promises.

Being a nice guy will just not do, an employee must have the relevant skills and the necessary training to do the job. Having natural talents and relevant gifts are even more desirable.

Successful companies take their time and go to great lengths just to find the most qualified persons for the jobs. They would rather hire costly and then manage easy afterwards. Just like the late Steve Jobs of Apple Inc. said:

> *"The secret to my success is that we've gone to exceptional lengths to hire the best people in the world."*

c) Positive energy

Another must have attribute for the new employees is positive energy. Being self-driven with a knack for achieving results should be a key determinant in the hiring decision.

A candidate should display a level of enthusiasm and positive attitude towards the job and the company's purpose.

Employees need to have inbuilt stamina or the staying power

to execute their assigned duties while simultaneously enjoying the work.

It can be quite frustrating to keep cajoling salaried staff to do their work; so save yourself the stress by hiring those who show a level of enthusiasm from the word go.

d) <u>Passion</u>

Passion is a big driver for staff productivity; it is the inner drive that keeps a person committed to a cause even if the circumstances are not so favorable. Your potential employees should therefore display a level of passion verifiable from their track records.

To build a super brand, you need an army of passionate foot soldiers who shall deliver the expected performance results come hell or high water.

The business environment has its fair share of upsets capable of disheartening average persons; you therefore need men and women who are passionate enough to keep pushing through with their commitments no matter what. You need people who do their duties for the love of it.

We have dedicated the next chapter to discuss this important attribute in depth.

e) <u>Cultural Fit</u>

Every successful organization either has an inbuilt culture that is supportive of the productivity levels the leadership favors or is in the process of building up such a culture.

When making hiring decisions therefore, hire those candidates who will easily make a good cultural fit. Such employees will not only bring positive energy to the team but would also want to stay.

Don't just hire people because they can do the job, on the contrary hire those who believe in what you also believe in, and they will naturally give you their best shot at driving the organizational mission. For such kind of individuals, your corporate mission becomes their mission too.

Just like author and speaker Simon Sinek said:

"If you hire people just because they can do the job, they will work for your money, but if you hire people who believe what you believe, they will work for you with their blood, sweat and tears"

Therefore during the hiring process do find out what drives your potential employees, what brings out the best in them and see whether it is in line with your corporate purpose, then make hiring decisions accordingly.

f) <u>Reliability</u>

Mistakes in business more often than not costs money. Such mistakes come in forms such as production of faulty products, bungled customer service and missed important deadlines, not to forget disappointed and unhappy customers.

You therefore need to work with people who are not only serious in their duties but are also attentive to take and duly follow instructions. Such employees will not only save the company unnecessary monetary losses but also facilitate opening of new revenue streams for the business.

Reliable employees will also easily take up additional responsibilities even those not directly within their job descriptions should there be need for such; equally they will always show up in time whenever called upon besides consistently delivering on their performance promises.

g) <u>Good communicator</u>

One of the vital skills that a new employee needs to have is good communication skills—oral and written. Communication essentially either makes or breaks a business.

You need staff members who can communicate in a lucid manner with their colleagues, customers and the management.

Inability to properly communicate can cause serious problems within an organization besides causing loss of valuable business opportunities and money.

Whereas, communication is a skill that can be sharpened, you will do well if you can hire and work with individuals who are talented communicators from the word go, persons who will only require a little sharpening from time to time especially for those in the front office and managerial roles.

Whereas there are many other role specific factors you could consider when seeking to hire the right persons, we are persuaded that the individuals who display a healthy combination of the aforementioned attributes will naturally fit in as valuable team members to drive your mission agenda. You can thereafter safely take care of training your new staff on any lacking job-specific skills.

As we **conclude** this chapter, we would like to end with a quote from American billionaire and business magnate Warren Buffet, on the qualities to look out for during the people selection process; Warren has emphasized on the importance of the first three attributes discussed above as follows:

> *"Somebody once said that in looking for people to hire,*
> *you look for three qualities: integrity, intelligence, and*

energy. And if you don't have the first, the other two will kill you"

Congratulations for reading this book up to this far, it indeed shows your desire to turn around your business fortunes. In the next chapter we shall cover a very important ingredient that drives the superior performances of the super brands, a virtue that its people possess with a royal generosity. Please read on to find out.

Reflection Questions

1)   What factors does your company consider to be critical when making hiring decisions?

2)   What would you say is the primary motivation of the staff members working in your establishment?

3)   The quality of the people that a company hires and retains is a fundamental game changer in the process of building a formidable business brand, what is your take on this?

CHAPTER FOUR: PASSION

*Tenacity to pursue brand's
purpose with a royal passion*

"The most powerful weapon on earth is the human soul on fire"

~FERDINAND FOCH

American writer, historian and philosopher William James Durant aptly remarked that ***"a nation is born stoic but dies epicurean."*** By which he meant that it takes great sacrifice and selflessness on the part of the nation's fathers to bring forth a new nation, but unfortunately the lethargy and the self-indulgence of the successive generations becomes the nation's ruin.

This statement could not be truer for every super brand that has had a significant impact in any industry. We could even borrow Will Durant's phrase and say that *a great brand is born stoic but dies epicurean.*

In this chapter therefore, we shall explore the fourth secret or pillar of the super brands that separates them from the pack, a quality that the members of every great organization possesses with a royal liberality:

> *The tenacity to pursue their purpose with unparalleled passion.*

Greatness has a lofty price that only a few people are willing to pay. Building a great brand takes hard work, sweat, blood and tears; there is a necessary sacrifice of inconvenience of time and money that must be paid for every ostensibly *overnight* success.

As a matter of fact, **growth and discovery are often accompanied by a certain degree of discomfort and uncertainty.** To push through all the inevitable challenges, discomforts and uncertainties in the pursuit of any worthy cause, you need to have passion.

What Then Is Passion?

Passion unfortunately is one of those words whose meaning has been diluted and mutated with the passage of time. Originally passion meant something entirely different. That original meaning and application is what this book refers to.

Today the word *passion* is associated with intense emotional desire towards an object or an activity. At least that's what the majority think it to be.

To start with, the word *passion* comes from the Greek word *passio* which means *to suffer* or *to endure*.

Passion originally meant *a willingness to suffer for what you love.* Passion therefore is a deep commitment to the subject of one's love to the extent of being ready to suffer for it.

Passion goes beyond mere enthusiasm and excitement. These are just part of and the external display of passion but not the crux of it thereof. Enthusiasm and excitement can be checked by the realities and changing circumstances in life; this is however not true for passion.

In this sense, the life of Jesus Christ on earth especially during the week of His crucifixion is what best exemplifies what passion actually means. The writer of the Bible book of Hebrews depicts the passion of Christ as follows:

> *...who for the joy that was set before him endured the cross, despising the shame, and is seated at the right hand of the throne of God.* **Hebrews 12:2** *(KJV 2000 Devotional Study Bible)*

In closer living memory, a man spent 27 of his best years locked up in prison for his conviction and steadfast determination to see a just nation where all citizens are treated equally without discrimination on the basis of their skin color. In his infamous Rivonia trial, it became clear that he was a man driven by passion to liberate his people from the clutches of apartheid, the possibility of facing the hangman's gallows notwithstanding.

This is the story of Nelson Mandela, the first black president of South Africa.

Here is an excerpt from his defense speech at the trial:

> *During my lifetime I have dedicated myself to this struggle of the African people. I have fought against white domination, and I have fought against black domination. I have cherished the ideal of a*

democratic and free society in which all persons live together in har-mony and with equal opportunities. It is an ideal which I hope to live for and to achieve. But if needs be, it is an ideal for which I am prepared to die.[1]

It is this kind of conviction that pushes great entrepreneurs to build their unique businesses. Similar passions drive entrepreneurs to see their ideals realized no matter the obstacles that they have to surmount or the hardships they have to endure.

That's why German Philosopher Georg Hegel rightly observed that:

> *"Nothing great in the world has been accomplished without passion"*

All the companies that have firmly established their signatures as formidable super brands have their inspiring stories to tell. They are stories of resilience, determination, hard work, blood, sweat, and tears on their journeys to greatness.

One enduring lesson we can gather from the various incidences of the remarkable success stories of the super brands is that:

> *If you are not willing to give up your conveniences and comforts to achieve your purpose, perhaps you don't want it strongly enough.*

The example from Equity Bank Ltd pioneer employees :

The author was privileged to be part of the pioneer team of Equity Bank Ltd (Kenya) employees, now a member of Equity Group Holdings, and witnessed firsthand the transformational power of passion at work.

In the financial industry then dominated by a few well established players, Equity bank team under the leadership of the indefatigable CEO James Mwangi burnt the midnight oil, sacrificed their time and conveniences, surmounted challenge after challenge in the noble pursuit to transform lives and bring dignity to the customers.

And the sacrifice paid off.

In less than two decades, Equity Group Holdings has become a financial powerhouse with a presence in over ten (10) African countries, effectively overtaking the other traditional players.

◆ ◆ ◆

Passion Is The Best Driver For Achieving Worthy Purposes In Life

Every great leader who has successfully navigated the murky waters of the business world has a story to tell.

They are heroic stories of triumphs over adversities; stories of resilience in the face of daunting setbacks; stories of moments of self-doubts and occasional burnouts; stories of disappointments, blood, sweat and tears in the singular pursuit of their worthy purpose. They are also stories of celebrations of remarkable milestones achieved in daunting circumstances.

From Oprah Winfrey, Jack Ma, Richard Branson, Donald Trump, Robert Kiyosaki, Warren Buffet, Strive Masiyiwa, Jeff Bezos, Elon Musk among others, all have had their fair share of failures and disappointments, moments of self-doubts and occasional burnouts; but they like all the other remarkable achievers in the various disciplines chose to shoulder on.

American pioneer industrialist and founder of Ford Motor Company, Henry Ford said that:

"When everything seems to be going against you, remember that the airplane takes off against the wind, not with it"

Pursuing any worthy cause is never smooth sailing. It takes real courage and unparalleled determination to stay on course come hell or high water.

To successfully steer the ship in boisterous seas with all the potential dangers and the occasional undercurrents working against you requires passion.

To turn your company vision into reality requires passion. You will of necessity meet obstacles and setbacks on the way; you will encounter disappointments and rejections in certain quarters, among other challenges. How you counter all these challenges and carry on will be a function of how passionate you are.

It therefore follows that teams or individuals who succeed in the face of these numerous challenges do so because they possess passion with royal liberality. Such is the case for all the leaders and employees of every leading brand that continue to grow by leaps and bounds.

Be that as it may, passion also entails having enthusiasm and excitement in the assignment you are undertaking.

The excitement that comes from an internal motivation puts real pleasure on the job.

When work is done with pleasure derived internally, perfection is always achievable. That's why legendary Greek Philosopher Aristotle said that:

"Pleasure in the job puts perfection in the work."

American business magnate and Co-founder of Apple Inc. the late Steve Jobs also said that:

"The only way to do great work is to love what you do"

A Leader's Passion Is The Business Magic Wand

For the leader, having a clear passion that others can tune into is the real game changer. ***A leader's contagious passion is a huge competitive advantage for the brand.*** If passion is necessary for the employees, it is critical for the leaders; for the leaders are also the brand's vision bearers.

It is almost impossible to build a great business brand without passion.

In this era of globalization, any business leader or entrepreneur lacking passion will be beaten hands down by someone else who is armed with passion.

Lack of passion will mean loss of valuable growth opportunities to the persons who are passionate enough and living elsewhere on the face of the earth. It is not fair but it is the reality.

Why Is Passion So Important For The Success Of The Brand?

In this section, we shall explore some specific reasons why you need passion for your business. These are some of the reasons:

    i.   *Passion begets creativity*
    ii.   *Passion sustains focus*
    iii.   *Passion triggers excellence*
    iv.   *Passion energizes people*
    v.   *Passion makes work enjoyable*

We shall discuss them hereunder:

    i.   *Passion begets creativity*

When you pour your passion into the pursuit of your purpose, you inadvertently provoke your creative mind and therefore easily come up with great ideas that can propel your brand to greatness. You become more innovative and hence you make faster progress.

    ii.   *Passion sustains focus*

When you are passionate about your core purpose, you will find it easier to eliminate distractions and disruptions that have the potential to dissuade you and derail your progress. All your energy and attention is focused only on what matters, which is the matter at hand.

It becomes easier to say no to every other suggestions or ideas that are not in line with your core mission.

    iii.   *Passion triggers excellence*

Passion and success are like Siamese twins; they are jointed at their core and always go together. If you put your best foot forward in the pursuit of your mission, excellence becomes the hallmark of your work and achievements.

This is so because your ground-breaking ideas from your creative center are more or less likely to be implemented much faster, with military precision to boot.

iv.   *Passion energizes people*

Passion is a source of inner positive energy that is also contagious; even in the face of temporary setbacks and seemingly insurmountable obstacles, passion will ooze boundless energy to keep you going. Your team will equally catch your zeal and commitment to your brand's purpose and will follow suit.

v.   *Passion makes work enjoyable*

Passion brings a spark of life to everything a passionate individual touches; this in turn brings fulfillment to the person and fun to the process.

Passion helps you to see the finished product upfront and thereafter helps you to connect every dot to the finished product; this makes every part of the process worthwhile however mundane or minimal it may be.

Passion enables you to love the work you do. Whereas it is enjoyable to do the work you love, it is much better to love the work you do.

We could go on and on but we are persuaded that the point has been made.

But just how do you cultivate passion in an organization? Let's read on to find out.

Rules For Cultivating Passion

The following are a few dos that when consistently practiced ensures there is contagious passion in the entire fabric of the organization:

- *Vision casting*
- *Recruit persons who share your vision*
- *Share heroic stories of triumph and achievements*
- *Reward creativity and excellence*
- *Use of automation and best practices in the business*

We shall discuss them below:

1. <u>Vision casting</u>

Your first role as a leader is to do vision casting. You need to clearly paint a mental picture of the organization's vision to your team members; endeavor to depict clearly how the envisioned future success will look like. It is your duty to help your team to see and appreciate the end or the outcome albeit only mentally.

French writer and poet Antoine de Saint-Exupery advised leaders on the best way to marshal teams to enthusiastically get involved in great undertakings. He said that:

"If you want to build a ship, don't drum up people to gather wood, divide the work and give orders. Instead teach them to yearn for the vast and endless immensity of the sea."

When you can present a compelling vision that properly engages the minds and hearts of the members of the organization, you will have succeeded to set their souls on fire.

When your team can clearly see the bigger picture and heartily embrace the company's worthy purpose, they will abandon themselves to the cause with all that they have. And the result shall be a shot at greatness.

2. <u>Recruit persons who share your vision</u>

People have different gifts, talents and callings in life. It therefore follows that not everyone can fit into your vision agenda. In order to get the best fit, ensure that you only recruit those persons who share your vision.

People who share your vision will not only be easier to work with but will also bring positive energy to the organization.

As already noted, don't just hire people because they can do the job, their inner drives in life is an important factor to consider in every hiring decision; this trait makes the difference between getting a splendid job done or getting ordinary performance results.

Just like motivational speaker and author Simon Sinek rightly observed that:

"If you hire people just because they can do the job, they will work for your money, but if you hire people who believe what you believe, they will work for you with their blood, sweat and tears"

3. <u>Share heroic stories of triumph and achievements</u>

Every institution has stories that can inspire passion and commitment to the organizational cause; these are heroic stories of courage or past conquests by the founders and the pioneer employees, stories of how seemingly insurmountable challenges were overcome in the past, stories of success and accolades in the days gone by.

Such stories instill firm beliefs on the employees' mindsets that they are in the right company of courageous men and women who are making history by acts of heroism and altruism; these stories further challenge the employees to live up to similar expectations.

Therefore make it a habit to share stories especially in staff trainings and other formal meetings. You can also document such inspiring stories and share the same in company newsletters to staff. The impact of such positive stories is undoubtedly huge.

4. <u>Reward creativity and excellence</u>

What gets rewarded gets repeated. By rewarding excellence and acts of creativity, you are passing a clear message on what you truly value as a business.

Who does not like being recognized and rewarded for their hard work, creativity and excellence?

You can give promotions based on individual's contributions and effort in furthering the mission of the company; you can also give certificates of excellence or merit for the same.

You can also consider giving trophies to departments or units that have demonstrated excellence in furthering the brand's purpose; financing team outings as rewards for registering milestones among other measures are also valid options.

5. <u>Use of automation and best practices in the business</u>

Automation of routine processes through technology and the use of best practices is another avenue for allowing people more time to concentrate on pursuing the brand's purpose.

Super brands routinely use systems and technology to take care of all the boring and repetitive stuff so as to release more time for the people to concentrate on what truly matters—pursuit of the brand's purpose.

Equally these great brands employ the best practices to encourage enjoyment of the work. Best-selling author and entrepreneur Daniel Priestley puts it this way:

Great entrepreneurs don't use systems, technology and best practices to get out of their business. They use them to get in deeper.[2]

As we come to the **end** of this chapter, we reiterate that without passion, a brand or a business cannot achieve much. As a matter of fact, companies actually begin to slide on a downward spiral the moment they let complacency and lethargy to set into their midst.

However when passion becomes a common thread shared by every team member, it becomes a source of synergy for great productivity that inevitably propels a brand to greatness and the enviable position of market dominance.

Equally, when passion becomes the hallmark of the organization, the employees get *pride of belonging* by associating with forward looking and dynamic brands. They look forward with eagerness to report to their duties every other day secure in the knowledge that their work makes positive impact in the world. This becomes a real productivity booster for any company.

It is therefore incumbent upon the leadership to ensure that this virtue is embraced by all the team members and sustained with increasing fervor at all times. We are persuaded that when you can consistently carry out the five practices discussed above, you will inevitably inspire passion within the entire fabric of the organization.

Now we move to the next secret of the super brands. Come with us to the next chapter.

Reflection Questions

1) A leader's passion is the business magic wand, what is your take on this?

2) To build a ship, French poet Antoine de Saint-Exupery advised that a leader should teach the followers to yearn for the vast and

endless immensity of the open sea; how can you practically implement a similar strategy in your establishment?

3) What is the current level of passion among your team members? In what practical ways can you enhance it?

CHAPTER FIVE: PRODUCTS

*Offering a suite of great
products that provide real
value to the Customers*

"Great companies are built on great products"

~ELON MUSK

Companies are in business either to provide some kind of solution to the society or to address particular pain points for specific constituencies within the society. In response to the identified needs that the company mission seeks to solve, various products are subsequently designed by the company to answer to those challenges in a commercially viable way.

Consequently, to build a great brand will of necessity require great products.

It is irrefutable fact that at the heart of every great company, there is a great product or a suite of superior products that provide real value to the target customers.

Being passionate while promoting or selling inferior or poor quality products and services will just not do; your business must of necessity provide real value to the customers through its products and services.

In the list of the secrets of the super brands, we have deliberately put product in the fifth position to emphasize an important point that there is more to building a super brand than just having products and services to sell.

Certainly great products that bring real value to the customers have their inalienable place in the process of building formidable business brands; nonetheless, great products and services are simply outgrowths of these other preceding factors.

As already noted in the foregoing chapters of this book, great brands are built in the relentless pursuit of higher purposes or nobler missions beyond the need to make some bucks for the business owners; furthermore in order to establish well-oiled productivity machinery, super brands typically employ unique business philosophies upon which both their day-to-day operations and the long term business strategies are firmly anchored; besides it takes a tribe of passionate enthusiasts comprising of dedicated teams of employees and hordes of evangelical customers to build a great brand.

Be that as it may, every super brand has a core product or a suite of products that it is known for.

> *It is simply impossible to build a successful business in the long run if there is no real value that the business adds to its customers.*

Even if you have the best sales staffs that are very passionate in giving the best customer experience, coupled with powerful business philosophies, you nonetheless still need to deliver real value to your customers through great products and quality services offering.

◆ ◆ ◆

What Then Is A Business Product?

A business product or service is a vehicle for delivering value to the customers. Business entities are in business to give value to their customers by solving their identified pain points or by giving them better alternatives to their existing solution mechanisms. The value or appropriate solutions are given to the customers in packages known as business products or services.

Simply put, *a business product or service is the vehicle or the consistent way through which a business entity delivers the desired outcome that their customers want.*

We shall validate this product definition using some examples from the leading business brands in different industries hereunder:

    i. *Sports gear manufacturer—Nike Inc. does not just sell sports gear; Nike delivers fashion statement to its consumers.*

    ii. *The Chinese Technology conglomerate—Huawei Company, does not just sell electronic gear and smart devices; Huawei expands the benefits of technology to everyone, everywhere.*

    iii. *The German Automobile manufacturer Mercedes-Benz does not just sell automobiles to its customers; Mercedes-Benz sells luxury, elegance and comfort to its customers.*

The singular focus of these super brands is on the desired outcome or results to be reaped by their customers as a result of consuming what the brands bring to the market.

We hope you get the difference.

Super brands are very clear about the real problem they are solving. And so should you. You need to understand that you are basically in business to do project managing of some sort of results for your customers.

Even if your business only offers services, the services must be structured in highly repeatable ways so as to resemble a product. It then becomes easier to name and brand such highly structured services just like you would name a physical product.

Structuring your service in a highly repeatable way can also be referred to as *productizing* the service.

◆ ◆ ◆

The Key To Product Success Is To Have A Workable Product Strategy

Quality products will build a formidable brand only when their design, production and distribution are approached from a well thought out product strategy.

It is not enough to have superior products and services, to truly make positive impact on customers and to disrupt the target market you must develop and use a workable product strategy.

What is clear from the onset is that the super brands do not sell a single product only; on the contrary super brands sell a suite of products. Super brands offer their customers what can be referred to as a *product eco-system.*

It is neither commercially viable nor profitable to rely on just a single business product however great that product might be.

The key to having insanely profitable businesses is to a have a suite of related quality products that can provide appropriate solutions to the customers' range of needs.

We will proceed hereafter to share with you some salient features of the product strategies of the industry titans that have set them apart from the pack.

Product Strategy Of The Industry Titans

Almost every super brand follows a product strategy whose pattern or composition we have decoded to include four basic steps or components:

1) *Free introductory gifts for the mass market*
2) *Inexpensive entry products for the prospects*
3) *Core product(s) for the customers*
4) *Supporting products that complement the core product(s)*

We shall explore these components in detail below:

1. <u>Free introductory gifts for the mass market</u>

Think of Google, Facebook, Twitter or even LinkedIn. These are all well-known valuable super brands. One of the most noticeable shared traits in the marketing approach by all these companies is that they give enormous value in quality products freely to the masses by design every year.

You probably have a social network account on Facebook, twitter or LinkedIn that you use to connect and communicate with your friends, peers and even your customers without having paid anything directly to the respective companies.

Products such as a basic LinkedIn account or internet search service using Google search engine or a G-mail account are all free gift products. Google Inc. even gives online maps and calendars for free.

These companies do not require any payment from customers to use these introductory products; neither do they obligate the users to buy the core products of the particular brands.

The purpose of these gifts is simply to warm the hearts of the prospective customers and to *'prepare'* them for possible brand-customer relationship in the immediate or the near future.

Giving of free gifts is such an ingenious way of marketing.

Other leading brands have followed the same route of giving free introductory gifts to the mass market. Let's take a few random examples to showcase this assertion:

    i.   *Apple Inc. gives consumers iTunes for free.*

    ii.   *Amazon Inc. allows authors to self-publish their books on their KDP (Kindle Direct Publishing) platform for free; even the KDP app is also downloadable from Amazon website free of charge.*

    iii.   *Equity Bank ltd (EBL) conducts mass financial literacy trainings for women and youth groups free of charge.*

    iv.   *Safaricom ltd gives new customers joining its network free SIM cards, at all their shops and dealer outlets countrywide (This was effective from November 2019)* [1]

The best defense of a working strategy is the abundance of positive results. Going by the results that these super brands continue to accrue from offering free but valuable introductory products to the masses, in terms of the huge numbers of new paying customers netted as a consequence thereof, is sufficient proof that the strategy works wonders.

You too need to seriously consider how you can give real value to your prospective and existing customers without always asking for payment in return. This introductory free value should be packaged as a gift to your prospective customers, a special product for your customers in line with your core purpose.

However, offering the free introductory gift should neither cost you an arm and a leg nor make your business to go bankrupt as a result thereof.

The gift could take various forms depending on the industry a business operates in such as:

- *A law firm could give free legal tips on particular legal subjects on a podcast or a regular blog.*
- *A chef or a restaurant could give out recipes for some special meals freely in a blog or a newsletter.*
- *A development and construction company could demystify the real estate development and construction processes with all the legalities involved in a newsletter or a YouTube channel.*
- *A medical doctor could give tips on early detection, prevention and management of some specific diseases in a podcast, YouTube channel or regular blog.*
- *A nutritionist could have a blog for healthy eating tips or free diet programs.*

<u>*Why you should give free introductory products:*</u>
Ideas are cheap nowadays; money is made in the implementation of ideas when you are assisting your customers to put the information into use. You might imagine that you are losing out by giving out too much information freely, but on the contrary you are creating a sea of prospective customers.

Giving out free products especially in the information economy earns you valuable credibility in the eyes of your prospects. It opens up the doors for the prospects to walk in and do business with your brand.

When these prospective clients decide to buy, your company becomes their go-to choice as they already have a taste of both your expertise and your valuable products.

This is how the super brands create huge unending funnels of prospective customers who are very eager to sign up as new paying customers; they do not have to spend an arm and a leg in marketing to register more sales.

Now, let's face some hard but interesting facts of business reality downtown folks:

- ✓ Chefs who regularly give out their recipes freely to prospects get more customers at their eateries week by week.
- ✓ Lawyers who give out free legal tips receive more enquiries and hence more customers as opposed to those who don't.
- ✓ Banks that offer free financial literacy trainings to the masses have more customers consuming their core products.
- ✓ A development and construction company that regularly deconstructs and demystifies all the legal jargon and the nitty-gritties of the development and construction industry either in a blog, newsletter or newspaper column gets more customers than those that don't.
- ✓ A physician who regularly shares updates on specific ailments on newspaper columns always have their private consulting clinics and hospitals full of new walk-in patients and referred customers.
- ✓ Mechanics or garages that regularly shares motoring tips on a blog or a newspaper column always have a steady stream of customers flocking their garages for motor vehicle maintenance service and repairs.

And the list goes on…

Just think about it, what would happen if Google decided to start charging customers for using its internet search engines! Or if Facebook opted to charge its customers for using the Facebook and WhatsApp applications!!

One thing is clear: many users would be locked out and the firms would lose considerable market value, not to mention that other players would come in handy to take advantage of the gap created therein to grow their own brands.

2. <u>Inexpensive entry products for the prospects</u>

The next component in the super brands product strategy is the use of inexpensive entry products for the prospects.

Those who have tasted or used the free gift product would be more or less inclined to take their journey with a brand a step further by either making further enquiries for possible purchase or displaying a willingness to be a customer. This is where the inexpensive entry product comes in as harbinger to the core product(s).

History has shown that once people have had a positive experience with free gifts that put them under no obligations to do business with a brand, the natural tendency is to warm up to that brand and be willing to commit a little by purchasing the brand's products but without spending too much either.

This is why a company needs to have an inexpensive entry product that gives the prospective customers a chance to do business with the brand albeit inexpensively.

These inexpensive entry products should of necessity provide real value to the customers without costing them an arm and a leg.

Many businesses rightly use these entry products to gather valuable data about their customers.

It should be noted however that the entry product should not be expensive to offer such that the business incurs loss as result of offering the same.

The example of Equity Bank Ltd (EBL)
EBL revolutionized banking in Kenya by shelving account opening charges and further scrapping the account maintenance ledger fees for all the accounts. This gave the masses that had hitherto been shunned by the other industry players, to open bank accounts without any further obligations to Equity bank.

Effectively the masses made EBL their home and choice bank. From these accounts Equity bank charged minimal transactions fees only on either cash transfers or cash withdrawals; deposit transactions were still largely been done free of charge.

You too should have some inexpensive products that you can use as a bait to get the prospective customers to further sample your range of solutions on offer. Your main aim here should be to gather customer data and get some level of commitment from your customers without making them to feel unduly pressurized by you.

Consider these examples as valuable leads:
- *A law firm giving a first one hour free consultancy service for new customers making enquiries at their offices.*
- *A nutritionist giving a healthy living booklet to the customers who subscribe to her blogs.*
- *A wedding planner giving a Checklist for a Memorable Wedding booklet to the couples making enquiries at her office or a downloadable version on the business website after the user has filled in some preliminary information in an opt-in online portal.*
- *A financial institution affording new customers to open savings or transaction accounts with very minimal or nil balances*
- *An hospital conducting free medical checkups for institutional customers*

NB:

As a pre-requisite for receiving the inexpensive entry product, the business must ensure that it gathers some preliminary customer information for possible follow up or future correspondence. This can be done by having customers sign in visitors' logbook, fill in query forms at the customer registration desks or complete online opt-in forms in case of online enquiries.

3. <u>The core product(s) for the customers</u>

At the heart of every business is a core quality product or products. Your core product is your main product; it is the product(s) that your business is known for.

Once your prospects have had a good experience with your appetizers—the free gifts and the inexpensive entry products, it is now time for the main course or the main meal—your core product(s).

Your core product(s) must of necessity be of high quality and should offer a remarkable solution to your ideal customers' problem.

Product quality is very important because a brand's reputation is greatly impacted by the quality of its products and services. Like someone aptly remarked that:

> *"Quality is remembered long after the price is forgotten"*

Your core product should resonate very well with your customers as to turn them into evangelists for your brand.

It should be noted that when prospective customers sample your free gifts or your inexpensive entry products, they instinctively weigh their options on whether to trust your brand as the ideal solution provider or not.

Potential customers are all over the place looking for answers or seeking solutions to their problems and pain points, your challenge therefore is to package your business products and services as the ideal solution to the customers' problems and pain points.

That's why digital analyst and author Brian Solis rightly observed that:

> *"The bottom line is that people are seeking answers and direction, not messages or sales pitches"*

The core product should therefore bring some real positive change to your customers.

It could be something you assist them to create or implement which they could not otherwise do or create on their own; or it could be a product they buy from you that will bring the desired positive outcome as envisaged. Either way using your core product should make your customers feel that it solved a problem or brought a huge benefit.

<u>*Your core product(s) should be your cash cow*</u>
The job of your core product is to make your business profitable. The price of the core product must therefore be right. You can afford to lose money on both the free gifts and the inexpensive entry products but not on your core product.

Unless yours is a charitable organization, you are in business to make money, lots of money. This means you must charge your core product appropriately to cover your costs and get a reasonable return on your investment.

Consider the list below for leads:
- *Giant Telecommunication Company Safaricom Ltd makes money on Voice and Data services, and it charges these main products well.*
- *Amazon Inc. makes money on online sales of third party products and they charge appropriately for the service.*
- *Mercedes Benz makes money from the sale of their state-of-the-art luxury automobiles, and their customers pay handsomely for these machines.*
- *Banks make money from credit and trade finance products, and these products are appropriately charged.*
- *Nutritionists and wellness coaches make money from working with their customers through the diet plans and wellness regimens respectively. And the price of these products is never cheap.*

You need to ask yourself whether your business has a core product that offers a solution to your customers' real problem; and whether that product is appropriately packaged and priced to give your business a reasonable return on your investment.

If the answer to the above question is not an emphatic yes, then it is time to design and appropriately package your core product(s) in line with your company purpose, so that you can make your business both commercially viable and profitable.

4. <u>Supporting products that complement the core product(s)</u>

This is the fourth component in the product suite of the super brands. Truly profitable brands add additional related products that naturally complement their core products.

Once you have won your customers and delighted them with your core product(s), new needs may still arise courtesy of consuming your core product(s) that will definitely require solutions. This is why you need other products that support or complement your core products.

These supportive products are mostly sold to the customers who have already purchased the core product(s).

The supportive products are usually very profitable since the cost of acquiring the customer is already covered.

Having supportive products also enables a business to have on-going working relationship with a customer for a long time to come.

A few examples will help to drive the point home:

> a. *The giant automobile manufacturer BMW has added Financial and Insurance services to its product eco-system; the German automobile super brand now sells insurance policies through its subsidiary BMW Group Financial services ltd, to the customers who have purchased their state-of-art cars be-*

sides handling the sale of their customers' old cars.

b. *Equity Bank Ltd (a member of Equity Group Holdings), a banking conglomerate in East and Central Africa, not only does insurance premium financing for its asset finance customers but also provide insurance policies for the same through its Equity Insurance Agency limited;*

c. *A fitness instructor who helps customers to lose weight could add personal image consulting to their business to assist clients who have consumed their core product.*

d. *An accountant who has given his customers tax return services could consider giving business coaching services as the additional product.*

As we come to the **end** of this chapter, we recap that super brands work with product strategy designed to take their customers on a journey that delivers positive experiences with the brand at every touch point; they typically approach their product strategy from an eco-system perspective.

By product eco-system, we mean that they sell different related products that solve their customers' problems and leave the customers feeling great that they did business with the respective brands.

Long before the prospects could consume their core products, they have either sampled the free gifts or some inexpensive trial products to get a feel of how the core product can be of benefit to them. The super brands then have their core products as well as other supporting products that come in handy in the list of their customer needs as a result of consuming the core products.

Just like best-selling author and business consultant Brian Tracy once said:

"You should approach each customer with the idea of

helping him or her to solve a problem or achieve a goal, not of selling a product or service"

Never attempt to build a super brand with only a single product however impeccable the product might be. You need a suite of products. You can borrow a leaf from these industry titans.

Now we can move to the next secret of the super brands. Let's turn to the next chapter.

Reflection Questions

1) It is impossible to build a great brand without providing real value to the customers. What unique value(s) does your business bring to the market?

2) What is your current product strategy? How does it compare with those of the industry titans?

3) Does your business have a known core product(s) that offers solution to the customers' real problem? How appropriate is your core product(s) packaged and priced?

CHAPTER SIX: PLACES

*Investing in Efficient products'
distribution systems*

*"A great product is nothing without a workable distribution chan-
nel"*

~RAGHAV HIMATSINGKA

In this chapter, we shall explore the sixth aspect of building a super brand—investing in efficient products distribution systems. This is the sixth secret or the sixth pillar of the super brands.

When you have in place a great product(s) or your productized service that gives the perfect solution to your identified client problems, you have made a laudable first step but it is not sufficient; you now need to have a workable product distribution system in place.

Ensuring adequate availability of your product(s) at the right places and at the right time to meet market demand is the second and most important component of a profitable product.

American internet entrepreneur and venture capitalist Reid Hoffman observed that:

> *"Having a great idea for a product is important, but having idea for product distribution is even more important"*

A great product is only profitable if the target customers can easily access it whenever and wherever they need it. Conversely, you may ask yourself **how good is a great product if the customers cannot access it whenever they need it!**

◆ ◆ ◆

Super Brands Invest In Marketing And Product Distribution Channels

Super brands invest heavily in their marketing and products distribution channels to both create sufficient market awareness and adequate product availability in all the places that the customers may need to access the product(s).

The reality on the ground is that a superior product with poor distribution network will unfortunately but invariably be overshadowed by an inferior product with good distribution network and easier customer access.

That's why Stephen Davis, the MD of CXO Advisory Group said that:

> *"An inferior product with better distribution will always*

win over a superior product with poor distribution or customer access. It's not fair. It's not right. But it's reality!"

A product will not just sell because it gives a superior solution to the customers' problems or because it brings a lot of good into the world; you must still have in place an efficient distribution mechanism and a great marketing strategy. Furthermore the product must be reasonably priced if it is to make any headway into the market and become sufficiently disruptive.

Invest adequately in your products distribution networks

In your specific business, you need to explore and invest in every cost-effective way to get your products and services to the customers. You should not lose out on sales simply because of poor product distribution mechanisms.

To start with you need to have beautifully designed brochures for your core products detailing the user benefits, which your sales and marketing team could then widely distribute to the target customers. Brochures are normally considered more authentic than the word of mouth from the sales persons.

Next, you need to have a well-designed user friendly website where your core products are properly described in a **FAB** *format*. FAB refers to product's *Features, Advantages and Benefits*. The website should also direct your prospects on how and where to access these products. Having an e-commerce platform on your website where you can do online sales for your core products would be a plus.

In case you are selling physical products you should have distribution stores in each of your target market areas where there is sizeable demand going by the volume of already registered sales and on-going prospects. Having your products well stocked by other retailers and wholesalers in the target locations is also a viable and cheaper option.

Listing your products for sale on other online e-commerce platforms such as e-*bay, amazon, Jumia* etc. or working in close partnership with online product distributors could also be a viable and cheaper option.

Let's consider two examples of great product distribution channels hereunder:

a)　*The product distribution networks of Safaricom ltd*
Safaricom Ltd is a leading telecommunication company in Kenya and the East African region. It has registered meteoric growth both in terms of active customer numbers and profitability since its inception in the year 2000.

Safaricom's phenomenal growth is largely attributable to its heavy investment in both efficient product distribution networks and infrastructural support systems.

Safaricom had a total of **5,314** network sites as at March 2020.[1]

This has enabled the giant Telco to have stronger and wider network coverage reaching even the remotest parts of the country.

Safaricom ltd has also opened customer service shops in almost every major urban center and every city across the country where the company not only sells authentic and quality merchandise such as smart phones, modems and laptops to its customers at affordable prices, but the firm also attends to customer service issues in these service centers in real-time basis. This is in addition to the Safaricom Call Centre in Nairobi that is operational 24/7.

Furthermore, Safaricom ltd has conscripted an abundance of multiple agents in almost every shopping center in the country, even in the far flung villages, to meet their customers' product and service needs.

Safaricom had a total of **173, 259** M-PESA agents country-wide as at March 2020.[2]

As a result of this widespread and excellent product distribution network and infrastructure support, Safaricom customers do not strain to buy airtime scratch cards or to look for network coverage. In terms of browsing capabilities, the company boasts of the fastest 4G network in the country as at the time of writing this book.

This singular focus on having efficient products distribution channels and products' support through investment in superior technological infrastructure has effectively propelled Safaricom ltd to the position of market dominance in telecommunications industry in the country and the region.

b) *Product distribution system of McDonald's*
The US based fast food giant McDonald's owes its huge success to its efficient product distribution system. McDonald's has perfected the art of having standardized cafes with superior and faster service in strategic locations where their customers easily access fast foods with very little or no hassles.

This is the strategic advantage and key to McDonald's phenomenal success.

Ray Kroc, the former CEO of McDonald's once said that:

"If man goes to the moon, we will go there too, open a restaurant and serve him a great burger at a great price."

To add icing to the cake, McDonald's also offers both take-aways and food delivery services to customers through its *McDelivery* service in partnership with *Uber Eats* and *Just Eat* apps[4]

◆ ◆ ◆

Customers Are Today Spoilt For Choices

In this era of cut-throat competition, customers will easily get alternatives to a particular product in case of product access challenges. The onus is therefore upon the brand to avail its products where it is most convenient for the customers to access it.

There is a time I went to buy some high school text books by a specific publisher as had been recommended by the subject teacher. I went to all the major book shops in town only to be disappointed that the books by this particular publisher were out of stock. The shop owners even advised me to buy alternative text books that could serve the same purpose. I finally managed to get the books I wanted from a faraway urban center but the experience was not pleasant at all.

I was not surprised to learn from the mainstream media a few months later, that the publisher in question had recorded huge financial loss for the same trading period. I will equally not be shocked if the same publisher goes under sooner or later unless they revise their *modus operandi* of marketing and products distribution.

Such out-of-stock stories do not augur well for brands that seek market dominance. It inadvertently creates a market perception of inefficiency and unreliability of the brand. In the end the brand will lose even its most ardent customers if their product needs cannot be met for long.

◆ ◆ ◆

Technology Has Made Product Distribution Easier

And Cheaper

For most industries such as the online retail and banking, technology has made product distribution and access easier and less costly.

Today a number of companies' products can be accessed from any part of the globe where there is internet connectivity through the companies *online access portals* or other e-commerce platforms such as Alibaba.com and e-bay.

The leading online retailer Amazon Inc. continues to play the role of a pacesetter in the online retail industry; Amazon e-commerce platform is accessible from any part of the globe where there is internet access and has become the preferred medium for self-publishers and other artists to sell their products.

Social media networks such as Facebook and LinkedIn are also accessible from anywhere where there is internet connectivity and are nowadays utilized by entrepreneurs to market their products.

In the same way, you too can leverage on the power of the internet to reach your customers wherever they can be on the face of the globe.

Be that as it may, regardless of the industry you operate in and the type of products or services you offer, you should of necessity leverage on the power of technology to give your customers easier access to your products and services.

As part of the product distribution strategy, super brands also employ the use of technology to give their customers more avenues to contact and connect with them easily at the customers' convenience. This kind of support greatly enhances the customers' experience with the respective brand.

If you are a financial institution, you need to have *POS* (point of sale) devices in strategic places such as the local superstores, fuel stations, hotels and other eateries, to enable your customers to do cashless transactions with their debit or credit cards. Furthermore the use of either *e-banking* platform or *mobile banking app* is now a must have for any serious banking brand.

If you are an insurance service provider, you need to invest in both mobile based and web based self-service application systems where customers can buy policies, make payments on the go and access their individual account statements on demand.

We could have many more examples depending on the nature of the business. We are however persuaded that the point has been made.

Rules For Investing In Profitable Distribution Channels

But just how should you determine how and where to invest in profitable distribution channels?

Hereunder we shall give you three cardinal rules you need to consider while investing in profitable distribution channels:

    i.   *Accessibility*

    ii.   *Convenience*

    iii.   *User-friendliness*

We shall discuss the same below:

    i.   *Accessibility*

The first point to consider is the ease of access of your products by your customers. You need to ensure that your products are adequately available wherever your customers can easily access them. Such product availability ensures that the market demand is appropriately met with sufficient supply at all times.

Your distribution network should therefore be informed by your customers' distribution and levels of market demand.

ii.   Convenience

The second factor is convenience. The whole point of having efficient product distribution is to bring convenience to your customers whenever they need the brand's products. Ensure your products' and services access is hassle-free as much as possible.

Technology has come in handy to aid in product distribution. Depending on your industry therefore, consider employing the benefits of technology to enhance your customers' convenience. This includes the use of technology apps, online purchase options, self-service retail outlets among others.

It is a win-win for both parties. Customers get to enjoy convenient access to your products and services while the companies get to register more profitable sales.

iii.   User-friendliness

The third factor is user-friendliness. Your distribution channels should be as user friendly as possible especially for the self-service portals or terminals.

Your customers are not all information technology gurus; therefore design the user interface of every service touchpoint for a layman's use. This goes a long way in enhancing the overall customer experience with a brand.

As we come to the **end** of this chapter, we would like to reiterate that super brands do not just produce superior products and stop at that, that they also invest in workable product distribution channels to get their products to wherever the customers are and whenever the customers need them.

Investing in workable product distribution systems is what makes the difference between making adequate and profitable product sales on the one hand, and low and unprofitable sales on the other.

Now we can move to the seventh and last secret of the super brands. Let's turn to the next chapter.

Reflection Questions

1) How efficient is your current products' distribution strategy?

2) How can your company leverage on technology to enhance your products' distribution channels?

3) A great product with inferior distribution strategy is invariably overshadowed by an inferior product with a superior distribution strategy. What is your take on this?

CHAPTER SEVEN: PARTNERSHIPS

The Art of Forging and Maintaining Valuable Partnerships

"Great partnerships thrive because the people need each other"

~COURTNEY A. KEMP

And now we come to the final secret of the super brands that sets them apart from the vast average companies—the art of forging and maintaining valuable partnerships.

Great brands understand that success is a function of team work; that great accomplishment is born out of collaborations with partners, allies and teams of dedicated individuals working together for the same objective.

Nothing of considerable value was ever a product of a single person's effort; on the contrary every landmark achievement is always the result of collaborative efforts of allies, teams and partners.

Actually creation is an act of collaboration. Nothing of significance that has stood the test of time was ever built by a single person.

◆ ◆ ◆

What Is Partnership?

Partnership is a formal arrangement between different parties to work together towards common goals; it entails collaborative efforts and cooperation between allies to achieve common objectives.

Partnership is about working together to achieve common objectives with the added benefits of synergy.

The spirit of partnership is a powerful driving force. It shifts our focus from only thinking about what is in it for me as an individual, to thinking about what is in it for all of us collectively as a group or for either party. The partnership mindset makes us to work together towards creating long-term success for everyone involved.

We hope you are familiar with the African proverb: *"If you want to go fast, go alone; if you want to go far, go together."* The adage is a call to collaborate with other likeminded persons in the spirit of partnership in order to achieve worthwhile goals in life.

Leading companies understand the power of partnerships as a valuable ingredient in the process of building successful business brands and thus relentlessly deploy the same to move ahead of the competition.

The example from the Bible

The epitome of God's creation, the creator's own masterpiece—man, was created through a collaboration of the Holy Trinity, and you can see and marvel at what man has been able to accomplish!

It is written in the book of Genesis as follows:

> *Then God said, "Let **us** make man in **our** image, in **our** likeness...."* **Genesis 1:26 NIV** *(emphasis added in bold)*

From that grand example, man took cue and noted that every magnificent and worthy assignment is done through a collaborative process; creating a winning business brand is by no means an exception.

◆ ◆ ◆

Building A Successful Business Brand Takes Valuable Partnerships

Building a company that makes meaningful impact in the world, a company that can withstand the test of time will of necessity require a network of allies, advisors, and partners. It is never a solo undertaking.

Learning to select the right partners and, in turn, trusting them is therefore an extremely vital skill for building a successful business brand.

Actually leading brands approach their business relationships with the lenses of partnership. These brands typically consider everyone who touches their businesses as partners. This mindset radically shifts their business approach away from the short-term transactional behavior prevalent in most average companies towards long-term relationships and success for everyone.

Whereas transactional engagements are geared towards reaping the maximum value out of an exchange in the immediate short-term, the spirit of partnership is about working together to create success and mutual benefits now and in the future.

Partnership therefore helps to create deeper alignment in the needs and wants of everyone who is interacting with the brand.

Building a successful company necessitates the need to strengthen every business component and the maintenance of healthy relationships with all the various stakeholders.

American entrepreneur and author Michael J. Saylor rightly remarked that:

> *"When you are building a company, you need to continually strengthen every component –finance, strategic partnerships, executive team, and relationships with every last constituency"*

◆ ◆ ◆

Your Business Success Is Dependent On Several Relationships

Your business is an entity whose survival is dependent on several relationships. And incidentally these relationships or partnerships must stay healthy if your business is to achieve and sustain success.

These partnerships take many forms such as:
1. *Partnership of the business co-founders or joint owners*
2. *Partnership with the employees*
3. *Partnership with the suppliers*
4. *Partnership with other brands*
5. *Partnership with the customers*

We will explore each of these partnership forms hereunder:

1. *Partnership of the business co-founders or joint owners*

This is perhaps the most obvious form of partnership. It is applicable where two or more persons with common business interest have pulled their resources together and jointly started a business. They thereafter manage the business and jointly share the profits and losses as per their terms of agreement.

Such partnerships survive because both partners recognize the valuable contributions of each other. Besides, these partners also complement one another with their different unique strengths and capabilities.

There are several examples of successful jointly founded businesses that have grown to become global brands. These include: [1]

i. Twitter, founded in 2006 by Evan Williams and Biz Stone
ii. Google Inc. founded in 1998 by Larry Page and Sergei Brin
iii. Yahoo! Founded in 1995 by Jerry Yang and David Filo
iv. Apple Inc. founded in 1976 by Steve Jobs and Steve Wozniak
v. Microsoft Company founded in 1975 by Bill Gates and Paul Allen
vi. Intel, founded in 1968 by Gordon Moore and Bob Noyce
vii. Hewlett-Packard (HP), founded in 1939 by Bill Hewlett and Dave Packard
viii. Procter and Gamble, founded in 1837 by William Procter and James Gamble

2. *Partnership with the employees*

This is the second form of vital partnership for a brand's success. Insanely successful brands treat their employees as partners in the business. In a number of cases, these businesses even give their employees stakes in the company ownership as part of their compensation.

Such companies appreciate the value of having totally committed employees who know they are also partly working for themselves, and thereby stand to grow together financially with the company as its net worth appreciates.

The spirit of partnership in these companies is further reflected in the fair human resource policies instituted for the employees and the atmosphere of collaboration and understanding prevailing at the work place.

This working relationship pays huge dividends to both parties. The brand gets to register phenomenal growth from its tribe of dedicated and zealous employees while the employees get to reap the benefits of sharing in the increased company fortunes.

Examples of this great company-employees partnership include:

i. Huawei Company which is wholly owned by the employees through ESOP (Employee Stock Ownership Plan). This position has been verified independently by Huawei's accountants, KPMG, who reported on Huawei's private ownership structure with **98.86** percent of the equity owned by employees and only **1.14** percent retained by Zhengfei.[2]

ii. *Equity Bank ltd (Kenya) now Member Company of Equity Group Holdings that also incorporated the employees into equity ownership through ESOP, in line with the Equity Bank's philosophy of 'Growing together in trust.'*

It should be noted however that treating your employees as your business partners does not always amount to co-opting them into the company share ownership. On the contrary, *the spirit of employer-employee partnership is exhibited on the fair and just treatment of the employees.* This is demonstrated through:

- *Reasonable terms of employment*
- *Fair and generous compensation programs*
- *Internal opportunities for employees' growth and develop-*

ment
- *Just and unprejudiced disciplinary policies etc.*

On the other end of the spectrum, you find most average or struggling companies that treat their employees more or less as cost centers instead of valuable partners on the same journey. The employer-employee relationship in these latter companies is characterized by:

- *The employees that are paid peanuts and/or are permanently casual.*
- *The employees are always the first casualties in case of business downturns.*
- *Penalizing the employees for every joint mistake that results into monetary loss for the company etc.*

In such circumstances, employee loyalty is non-existent; and there is usually a higher staff turnover and subsequent higher staff replacement costs.

3. *Partnership with the suppliers*

The other critical constituency that a brand needs to relate with in a cordial partnership arrangement is the suppliers.

Every business desirous to build a distinguished brand needs to have dependable suppliers with which it shares common values of high quality standards and uncompromising integrity.

In response to such virtues, it behooves the brand to return the favor by treating these suppliers as valuable partners of the brand. This is done by paying the suppliers promptly for the supplies received from them and extending to the partners any benefits that could further enhance the cordial working relationship.

Having cordial supplier-company relationship ensures that the business always gets the best quality supplies on an ongoing basis. This in turn enables the company to make superior quality products for its customers or to offer superior quality services to the same.

Huawei founder and rotating CEO Ren Zhengfei captured this understanding powerfully in his report on supply situation to Huawei Company as follows:

> *When a company grows to a certain size, it must build strategic partnerships with its suppliers to ensure the ongoing supply of materials and components. This is also necessary for the company to develop rapidly.*[3]

It is important to note that your suppliers are also in business probably facing similar economic conditions; they therefore look up to you to promptly honor your debt obligations so as to help them manage their cash flows well.

Besides, building good credit history with your suppliers will earn you better credit terms and great discounts, which is an automatic boost to your revenues and hence the bottom line.

Your business suppliers are like the tributaries of a big river, the continued flow of the river is largely dependent on the sustainability and strength of its tributaries. It pays to ensure that you keep your tributaries properly functioning by honoring your obligations to them, and promptly releasing the payments for the supplies received from them.

Indeed it is in your best long-term business interests to keep cordial working relationship with your suppliers.

Ultimately it is simply self-defeating to treat your suppliers like competitors with a hostile attitude to boot. As your suppliers begin to suffer cash crunches due to huge unpaid debts owed to them by your business entity, you will inevitably receive damning publicity from the disgruntled suppliers' acts of desperation, and could further face ruinous industrial actions. None of these is good for your brand's reputation.

A number of superstores and other corporations have faced ruinous litigations from their suppliers in the recent past, owing to huge unpaid debts. This has forced some of the affected companies to be put under receivership, with others being liquidated altogether in the process.

4. *Partnership with other brands*

Businesses normally combine forces with other brands in similar or related fields in order to venture into new business segments or make inroads into new market territories. This is done through strategic partnerships driven primarily by symbiotic considerations.

The use of strategic partnerships is by far the fastest way to grow a brand's market share by tapping into the unique strengths, competencies and existing customer base of the partner businesses.

No single business can profitably survive for long as an island. With time the managements of various companies will find it necessary to join forces with likeminded others to leverage on their unique capabilities or to build bigger war chests.

Some companies tend to favor mergers and acquisitions as their preferred growth strategy, other companies prefer to work as allies or partners to achieve similar goals.

Great entrepreneurs and business persons usually work as allies with one another. They don't let their rivalries degenerate into enmity; on the contrary they capitalize on the things that unite them such as shared business interests, rather than focusing on the things that divide them.

Moreover, great entrepreneurs always seek for ways to mutually enhance their service delivery to their shared customers. In the process, each brand grows their customer base, increases sales turnover and grows their wallet sizes.

◆ ◆ ◆

The example of strategic brand partnership: a case study of Safaricom _ltd_

The giant Telco, Safaricom ltd has used the power of valuable brand partnerships to unlock new growth opportunities and cement its leadership position in the telecommunication industry in the East Africa region. From content creation, to product and infrastructural development, Safaricom is always on the lookout for allies and partners to work with in realizing their shared objectives.

In its annual sustainable business report for the year 2019, the firm reported as follows on their partnership endeavor:

> _"We continue to work with US tech giants Amazon and Microsoft to drive a number of areas of innovation, co-creating new products and building capacity."[4]_

Safaricom considers strategic business partnerships such a critical success factor that cannot be ignored by any one sector—public or private. In the same referenced 2019 business report, Safaricom avers that:

> _The truth is, no one sector – public, private or NGO – has the capacity to address the fundamental business and social challenges that we face today. And that is why collaborative and inclusive approaches to business and cross-sectoral partnerships are critical[5]_

The following are some specific examples of partnerships of Safaricom ltd with other brands both locally and internationally[6]:

i.   _M-Gas IoT solution for low-income households_
This is an innovative clean cooking gas solution from Safaricom ltd in partnership with M-Gas Company, targeting customers who cannot otherwise afford to raise the initial cost of cooking gas kit.

The partnership enables this category of customers to access clean and environmentally friendly but affordable energy for cooking in their households without paying for the M-Gas kit. Customers get M-Gas kit comprising of 13 Kg gas cylinder with a 2-burner cooker at no upfront cost.

The gas cylinder is equipped with an innovative smart meter that shows the amount of gas for which a customer has paid and how much fuel they have remaining.

Customers have the flexibility to purchase any amount of gas. The gas automatically disconnects when the available balance paid for has been consumed. However, top-up payments for more gas can be made easily and conveniently through Safaricom's M-PESA app.

The cost of providing three meals for an average household is estimated to cost less than $1 per day and is therefore within the reach of majority of the households especially those living in the slum areas.

ii. _Partnering with Amazon to accelerate the roll-out of cloud services_

Safaricom ltd is the pioneer Amazon Web Services Advance (AWSA) consulting partner in East Africa. This partnership is meant to help local enterprises to take advantage to the very latest technologies in the world without having to buy, maintain and upgrade expensive physical data centers and servers.

iii. _Partnership with Google to digitize customers_

This partnership is meant to enable more Safaricom customers to transition to smart devices and enjoy digital experience through the purchase of highly subsidized low-priced smart phones—_Neon Ray (4G)_ and _Neon Storm (3G)_

This partnership enables Google Inc. to increase sales of their smart phones while Safaricom ltd gets to increase its revenue from mobile data consumption as more customers are enabled to access internet connectivity via their phones hence more internet browsing.

iv.   *Partnership with M-Kopa Solar to enable customers to buy high end devices through check-off system*

This partnership allows more Safaricom ltd customers to buy high end smart devices through a daily payment arrangement of Kes 40 via check off system.

This partnership effectively increased the number of smart phones connected to Safaricom network by 23% to 15 Million and 4G enabled smartphones increased by 91% to 6.1 million by March 2020.

v.   *Partnership with BuuPass for digital travel booking experience*

Safaricom also partnered with *BuuPass*, the innovative online bus, shuttle and train booking service application to allow passengers to book for their travelling on their transport company of choice and pay for their tickets using M-PESA.

Customers can access the service by dialing *877# or visiting buupass.com and payments for tickets are accepted through M-PESA.

This partnership has brought a lot of convenience to travellers. Through *BuuPass*, customers can select a bus or a shuttle operator, their preferred travel date and time, and reserve specific seat numbers. Customers can also reserve seats for multiple travellers, with tickets printed at the bus station after presentation of the confirmation SMS from *BuuPass*.

vi.   *M-Pesa Global*

Safaricom has firmly set its focus to become a major player in the money transfer services by launching M-Pesa Global service. This is an innovative service that enables Safaricom M-

PESA registered customers to send and receive money from many countries across the world, in partnership with Western Union, MoneyGram, Wave, Ria, WorldRemit, Remitly among others.

This service has continued to gain momentum since its launch in 2019. The service contributed kes 1.3 Billion in Safaricom revenue in 2020, and was estimated to contribute more than 50 per cent of all inbound diaspora remittances to Kenya in the same year.

❖ ❖ ❖

Let's look at additional examples of symbiotic brand partnerships:

i. The giant online retailer Amazon recently partnered with American Express, a credit card company, to improve on the way small businesses sell on their platform and to provide enhanced data insights on their purchasing activities. Both companies now have a co-branded credit card for their customers.[7]

ii. McDonald's has partnered with technology companies *Uber Eats* and *Just Eat* to offer food delivery services to customers through its *McDelivery* service. McDonalds makes the delicious dishes and *Uber Eats* and *Just Eat* delivers the same to the customers who requests for the service through these technology apps[8]

iii. In Kenya, Equity Bank ltd partnered with Airtel ltd— a telecommunication company to enable each brand to ride on the unique capabilities of each other.

Equity bank customers got to enjoy the benefits of cheaper and convenient mobile banking through their co-branded Equitel lines while Airtel ltd got to tap into the huge Equity bank customer base, even as their own customers enjoy modern banking services at their fingertips.[9]

iii. Banking institutions such as Kenya Commercial Bank and Equity Bank Ltd normally partner with credit card companies such as Visa and MasterCard to enable their customers enjoy the benefits of cashless transactions at point of sale terminals in the supermarkets, gas stations, some eateries and hotels etc.

In your business, be on the look-out for other businesses or brands with which you can join forces in symbiotic relationships. **You may not be on the same boat but you are definitely facing the same storm.** Why not join forces together and travel in larger ships that can withstand the boisterous sea?

Be the entrepreneur who looks out for the things that unite more than the things that divide. Your brand will grow match faster when you find strategic partners to work with.

5. *Partnership with the customers*

This is perhaps the best partnership a brand can ever have—*the long-term patronage and loyalty of customers.*

This is only possible when a brand truly creates value for its customers; when a business truly understands the customers' needs and their pain points, and avail to them products and services that provide ideal solutions to those problems.

Even more importantly, you need to note that customers only become your partners when they can feel you; when they know that you truly care about them and recognize them as individuals who add value to your business.

They become partners when they are persuaded that you understand their needs and pain points and that you are willing and ready to walk the journey with them to address those challenges.

Moreover, customers give their loyalty and continued patronage to a brand when they believe that the brand puts their interests ahead of its own profitability objectives.

In other words customers only become your partners when they can trust you.

Trust is the magic key to win the customers' loyalty and continued patronage. There is just but one way to satisfy and maintain good customer relationships and earn the customers' trust, and that is to provide premium services.

Offering premium services or superior customer experience will invariably result in our customers being delighted and amazed with our products and service quality long after they have transacted with us. Such service will not only make customers to commend us in their circles of influence but will cause them to joyfully look forward to doing repeat business with us.

NB:
For more information on superior customer experience, get a copy of the book by the same author, entitled *Superior Customer Experience: The New Business Brand.*

Rules For Formulating Valuable Partnerships

But just how do you form valuable or strategic partnerships?

Just like any other relationship, business partnerships are cultivated over time. You therefore need patience and understanding as you work out on any business relationship.

Every enduring and strategic partnership has incorporated these four aspects:

- *Mutual benefit*

- *Respect for one another*
- *Common understanding*
- *Mutual trust*

Let's explore them hereunder:

i. *Mutual benefit*

Partnerships thrive because the parties involved recognize that they need each other for their continued reciprocal advantages. Each and every party involved must gain from the partnership. In other words, it must be a win-win arrangement where each party works for the long term benefit of each and everyone involved.

This implies that for the success of every partnership, the relationship must be symbiotic in nature where each party brings real value to the other and together all the partners reap the benefits of synergy.

ii. *Respect for one another*

Respecting the unique differences and capabilities of each other is the cornerstone of every long-term relationship. Healthy partnership requires taking into consideration each other's perspectives and honoring their differing points of view.

Differing opinions between partners do not have to become contentious grounds for conflicts; on the contrary, partners usually look for common grounds for compromise and amicable resolutions.

In the end, true partnership spirit will mean covering each other's weaknesses or shortfalls while majoring on their strong areas.

Equally, partners need to know that they are both valued and needed by each other.

iii.   Common understanding

Thriving partnerships are anchored on a solid base of common understanding on such issues like purpose, expectations, objectives and boundaries.

Partnerships work well when there are clear expectations or terms of engagement between the parties involved from the word go.

Every participating partner should be clear on their roles and responsibilities to each other and to the partnership in general.   Any grey area left unclarified potentially becomes a possible conflict ground in a partnership setting sooner or later.

It is therefore advisable to have a written agreement witnessed by an attorney, not necessarily to protect yourself from each other but in order to remain true to every partner's obligations.

Having a verbal or informal arrangement between partners or simply assuming that every partner understands their obligations and will live up to the expectations of each other is a recipe for great conflicts and the eventual death of the partnership.

iv.   Mutual trust

Whereas respect for each other is the cornerstone of every working partnership, trust is the bedrock of the same. Mutual trust is so essential for the purpose of sustaining business partnership that once it is breached, the partnership is doomed.

Mutual trust is essential especially in resolving complications and difficulties when they do arise, and such complications occasionally do come up.

Suspicions in a partnership are like a virus that attacks a body, unless it is dealt with promptly, sooner or later it causes the death of the host body. You therefore need to protect the partnership from the opportunistic deadly viruses by immunizing yourself through building of mutual trust.

Whereas building trust takes time, it is worth every effort. What is needed in the process is goodwill and utmost good faith from either party that is involved in the partnership.

As we come to the **end** of this chapter, we reiterate that its pays huge dividends to form and maintain strategic partnerships with all the parties that touch your business in one way or another.

It is through these valuable partnerships that brands break into new territories, penetrate new market segments and eventually rubberstamp their authority in the market as formidable players in their particular industries.

Reflection Questions

1) Creating a winning business brand is a function of a collaborative process. What is your take on this?

2) Leading brands treat their employees, suppliers and customers as business partners, what is the current practice in your establishment?

3) Long term patronage and loyalty of customers is the best form of partnership a brand can have. This is however only possible when customers trust your brand. In what ways can you build customer confidence in your brand and win their trust?

4) How can you enhance and strengthen strategic partnerships and relationships with all your business stakeholders in practice?

CHAPTER EIGHT: WHAT NEXT?

"Knowing is not enough, we must apply. Willing is not enough, we must do."

~BRUCE LEE

The Hidden Theme

At the beginning of this book, we said that we shall be continuously referring to a consistent theme that all these ingredients collectively feed and serve. We preferred to hide it in plain sight throughout the book so that you can figure it out by yourself.

Most people read the book the first time and get it, others get it in their third reading, and still others don't just get it. We are however persuaded that you will get the most value out of this book once you *find and grasp* this hidden theme, and its exact application will inevitably revolutionize your business and turn it into a formidable brand.

Be that as it may, you can still apply the knowledge and wisdom of the sages gleaned from the pages of this book, to your great advantage.

As legendary martial arts supremo Bruce Lee once said:

> *"Knowing is not enough, we must apply. Willing is not enough, we must do."*

Information gleaned from this book will only be of benefit to those souls who will make use of them by applying the same in their businesses and organizations.

Statistics show that only a small fraction of people truly apply the knowledge they gather from the various sources to improve their lives and circumstances. You can purpose to be in that minority group of the doers and see your circumstances turn around.

◆ ◆ ◆

It Is Time For Action

You now have the seven secrets (7 Ps) of the super brands. You have seen what makes these industry giants to continue to dominate their industries. We trust that you have noted how these ingredients work in tandem to elevate the various businesses applying them into positions of market dominance and super profitability regardless of their industries and geographical locations.

We strongly believe that you have also noted that all the seven ingredients are very practical tenets and fortunately non-mystical; that they are all ideas and precepts that any entrepreneur or leader can apply to grow his or her business brand to greatness in its industry.

Perhaps the only magical thing in all these is the passion and persistence with which these super brands apply the ingredients and the success that ensues to them with exactness every time as a consequence thereof.

Possibly you may need help or support in implementing these ingredients in your organization; or you may require more information on the aforementioned issues. You can contact us and we will be both delighted and honored to partner with you on your journey of turning around your business into a formidable brand.

We are a team of experts drawn from various professions that work together to assist clients to unlock their full potential for growth and profitability, hence achieving greatness and prestige that comes with it. We do this through our consultancy firm—*Hezma Ventures Consulting.*

◆ ◆ ◆

About Hezma Ventures Consulting

Hezma Ventures Consulting is a premier leadership development and business management consultancy firm based in Kenya.

Our Purpose

We exist to assist corporations unlock peak productivity, enhance operational efficiencies and increase their profitability sustainably

Our Mission
We work with leaders and teams to create powerful cultures of excellence that spur enjoyable peak performances with reduced operational costs hence higher profits

We do this through captivating programs that aligns the hearts and minds of our clients' staff with their company purpose. This results in having highly engaged, proactive and productive teams actively delivering premium returns for the client companies.

Our Vision

To become a world class consulting powerhouse positively contributing to the development and prosperity of individuals and organizations

Our contact information

You can contact us through any of the following:

Postal address: P.O Box 2262-50200 Bungoma, Kenya
E-mail: info@hezmaventures.co.ke; hezmaventures@gmail.com
Telephone: +254 723 440 148/ +254 724 572 472
WhatsApp: +254 723 440 148

Facebook page: Hezma Ventures

Or visit our website at https://www.hezmaventures.co.ke

REFERENCES

Chapter One

1. About Nike at https://www.nike.com/help/a/nikeinc-mission accessed on December 15, 2020
2. About Nike at https://www.nike.com/help/a/nikeinc-mission accessed on December 15, 2020
3. Purpose statement of Nike Inc. available at https://purpose.nike.com/ accessed on February 17, 2021
4. Walmart 2017 annual report, page 5, available at https://s2.q4cdn.com/056532643/files/doc_financials/2017/Annual/WMT_2017_AR-(1).pdf accessed on February 16, 2021
5. Ron Ashkenas, Brook Manville (2018), 'The Harvard Business Review Leaders' Handbook" Harvard Business Review Press
6. Aziz, Afdhel (2020), The power of purpose, Forbes.com, available at https://www.forbes.com/sites/afdhelaziz/2020/02/18/the-power-of-purpose-the-7-elements-of-a-great-purpose-statement/?sh=748d77cb3fad accessed on December 15, 2020
7. Equity Group Holdings Purpose, available at: https://equitygroupholdings.com/ke/about-equity accessed on December 19, 2020
8. Purpose statement of Coca-Cola Company available at: https://www.coca-cola company.com/company/purpose-and-vision accessed on December 19, 2020
9. Kenya Commercial Bank group purpose statement, available at https://ke.kcbgroup.com/about-us accessed on

Dec 19, 2020

10. Safaricom purpose statement, Safaricom Sustainability Report 2016, page 5

11. Purpose of Zappos.com available at https://www.zappos.com/about/ accessed on Jan 2, 2021

Chapter Two

1) Huawei's Core Values, 2007

2) Samsung group philosophy available at https://www.samsung.com/us/aboutsamsung/vision/philosophy/philosophy-goals/_accessed on December 15, 2020

3) Brand finance global 500 2020 report, Page 11

4) Brand finance global 500 2020 report, Page 14

5) Huawei business philosophy, available at https://www.huawei.eu/who-we-are/our-philosophy accessed on December 15, 2020

6) Martin, Roll (2018), Huawei—Transforming a Chinese Technology Business to a Global Brand, available at https://martinroll.com/resources/articles/strategy/huawei-transforming-chinese-technology-business-global-brand/ accessed on December 18, 2020

7) Brand Finance Global 500 Brands 2020 report, page 8

8) Tesla's purpose, available at https://www.tesla.com/about accessed on December 18, 2020

9) Dudovskiy J. (2018) "Tesla Organizational Culture: a brief overview" Research Methodology, available at https://research-methodology.net/tesla-organizational-culture-a-brief-overview/ accessed on December 18, 2020

10) Bariso, Justin (2017) email from Elon Musk, Inc.com available at https://www.inc.com/justin-bariso/this-email-from-elon-musk-to-tesla-employees-descr.html accessed on January 18, 2021

11) Amazon's principles available at https://www.aboutamazon.com/about-us accessed on December

19, 2020

12)   Huang, Weiwei (2019): Built on value: The Huawei philosophy of finance management, Palgrave Macmillan, Singapore, Page 7

13)   Huang, Weiwei (2019): Built on value: The Huawei philosophy of finance management, Palgrave Macmillan, Singapore, Page 23

14)   Core values of Zappos.com available at https://www.zappos.com/about/what-we-live-by accessed on January 2, 2021

15)   Safaricom Sustainable Business Report 2020, Page 18, available at https://www.safaricom.co.ke/sustainabilityreport_2020/ accessed on February 7, 2021

16)   Safaricom Sustainability Report 2016, page 11 available at https://www.safaricom.co.ke/sustainabilityreport_2016/ accessed on February 7, 2021)

17)   Safaricom Sustainability Report 2016, page 21 available at https://www.safaricom.co.ke/sustainabilityreport_2016/ accessed on February 7, 2021)

18)   Huawei's Core values, available at https://www.huawei.eu/story/our-core-values-essence-huawei accessed on December 18, 2020

19)   Huang, Weiwei (2019): Built on value: The Huawei philosophy of finance management, Palgrave Macmillan, Singapore, Page 6

20)   Brand Finance Global 500—2020 report, page 14

21)   Massanari, Adrienne (2003), Work hard. Have fun. Make history. [Make money.]: Narratives of Amazon.com, University of Washington, page 13

22)   Samsung's Philosophies and goals, available at https://www.samsung.com/us/aboutsamsung/vision/philosophy/philosophy-goals/ accessed on December 20, 2020

Chapter Four

1) Mandela, Nelson (1994), The Long Walk to Freedom: The Autobiography of Nelson Mandela, Little, Brown and Company, page 215

2) Priestley, Daniel (2013), Entrepreneur Revolution, Capstone Publishing Ltd, West Sussex (UK), Page 107

Chapter Five

1. Safaricom sustainable business report 2020, Page 59, available at https://www.safaricom.co.ke/sustainabilityreport_2020/ accessed on February 7, 2021

Chapter Six

1) Safaricom sustainable business report 2020, Page 18, available at https://www.safaricom.co.ke/sustainabilityreport_2020/ accessed on February 7, 2021

2) Safaricom sustainable business report 2020, Page 18, available at https://www.safaricom.co.ke/sustainabilityreport_2020/ accessed on February 7, 2021

3) Priestley, Daniel (2017), Key Person of Influence, (Revised Edition) Rethink Press, Great Britain Page 74

4) McDonald's food delivery services, available at https://www.mcdonalds.com/gb/en-gb/latest/mcdelivery.html accessed on January 14, 2021

Chapter Seven

1) Brandt Ranj, Shontell Alyson (2016), 10 Insanely Successful Co-founders and why their partnerships worked, Business Insider.com available at https://www.businessinsider.com/10-successful-cofounders-and-why-their-partnerships-worked?IR=T accessed on December 19, 2020

2) Huang, Weiwei (2019): Built on value: The Huawei philosophy of finance management, Palgrave Macmillan, Singapore,

Page viii

3) Huang, Weiwei (2019) : Built on value: The Huawei philosophy of finance management, Palgrave Macmillan, Singapore, Page 66

4)   Safaricom sustainable business report 2019, Page 55, available at https://www.safaricom.co.ke/sustainabilityreport_2019/ accessed on February 7, 2021

5)   Safaricom sustainable business report 2019, Page 87, available at https://www.safaricom.co.ke/sustainabilityreport_2019/ accessed on February 7, 2021

6)   Safaricom sustainable business report 2020, Pages 53 and 54, available at https://www.safaricom.co.ke/sustainabilityreport_2020/ accessed on February 7, 2021

7) Amazon business at https://www.amazon.com/Amazon-Business-American-Express-Card/dp/B07984JN3L

8) McDonald's food delivery services, available at https://www.mcdonalds.com/gb/en-gb/latest/mcdelivery.html accessed on January 14, 2021

9) 6. Equity, Airtel partner to offer mobile services, available at https://www.theeastafrican.co.ke/tea/business/equity-airtel-partner-to-offer-mobile-services--1338668 accessed on January 14, 2021

ABOUT THE AUTHOR

Willis Amach

Willis Amach is a minister of the Word of God, Corporate trainer, Management and Leadership Consultant and Service Excellence Enthusiast.

He is the founder and lead Consultant at Hezma Ventures Consulting; a consultancy firm that works with leaders and teams to create powerful cultures of excellence that spur enjoyable peak performances with reduced operational costs hence higher profits for the client firms.

Check his full profile at https://www.amazon.com/~/e/B092PC-NGFH

BOOKS BY THIS AUTHOR

Superior Customer Experience: The New Business Brand

In today's extremely competitive market with an upsurge of commoditized products and services, increasingly informed and demanding customers; and stringent regulatory business environment plus intolerant shareholders to boot, running a profitable business is easier said than done.

Fortunately, there is an invaluable time tested and proven way for building insanely profitable businesses no matter the state of the economy and prevailing cutthroat competition. It all boils down to Offering Superior Customer Experience to your customers. Amazing Customer Experiences turns customers into brand evangelists actively advocating for the brand in their circles, and resulting into more profitable cost-effective sales.

In this book, we show you how to build a vibrant customer-centric culture that ensures awe-inspiring and seamless product and service delivery systems to a steadily growing pool of evangelical customers. With relevant examples and case studies, the book is rich with practical steps for turning any business into service excellence hub and insanely profitable enterprise.

Your customers are waiting.

Break Through The Barriers: Shatter Your

Limitations

Every person at one time or another has had dreams of doing something great with their lives, but not many people have mastered the courage to pursue those dreams. Many people continue to live in very deprived conditions despite the enormous potential and God-given capabilities packaged within them; they just do enough to get by and possibly arrive safely at the graveyard.

The few that make a positive difference in this world and live their lives to the fullest—those who master the courage to do what the rest are afraid to do, are the ones who have developed their inner persons to the point of breaking through the life and environmental barriers; and shattering the limitations imposed on them by personal deficiencies, culture and traditions.

Success is not for the chosen few; rather it is for the few who chose. This is the call to every living person today and the challenge posed by this book to choose success and embark on their journey to greatness. Time and circumstances have never been so ripe as it is now, for every individual to break the barriers and pursue their dreams and their life aspirations.

Experiencing Victorious Kingdom Life Now: Victory To Victory Everyday

The subject of the Kingdom of God is primarily the message of the gospel. The Gospel is about the King of Kings and the coming Kingdom. This was the core message of the LORD Jesus Christ. Though lost to the contemporary Christian, it is the good news that Jesus Christ came to proclaim. It is the gospel that the apostles of the early Church proclaimed.

This book seeks to reintroduce this lost gem to the hurting and disillusioned world with a waning Christian Influence. The author traces this concept from the very beginning of time, to when and how it was lost and how to rediscover and appropriate its full benefits here and now, and live victoriously every day.